Roman Provincial Wall Painting of the Western Empire

edited by

Joan Liversidge

B A R International Series 140

1982

B.A.R.

B.A.R., 122 Banbury Road, Oxford OX2 7BP, England

GENERAL EDITORS

A. R. Hands, B.Sc., M.A., D.Phil.
D. R. Walker, M.A.

B.A.R.-S140, 1982: 'Roman Provincial Wall Painting of the Western Empire'.

© The Individual Authors, 1982.

ISBN 0 86054 171 1

Printed in Great Britain

CONTENTS

INTRODUCTION

Joan Liversidge

'The walls of some of the rooms appear to have been ornamented with a ground of rich red, divided into panels by borders of various colours, in which were interspersed birds, flowers, stars and fanciful objects.'[1] Thus wrote the excavator of a Romano-British villa in 1848, a description which might apply to many a Roman provincial site.

In this case, too, a few fragments of the painted walls still survive to bear out the account. Such scanty evidence with brief records is typical of many older discoveries, and as painted plaster does not have the durable quality of mosaic floors, this important decorative element in provincial buildings has been largely ignored.

During the last twenty years, however, the situation has changed dramatically. Improved methods of excavation now frequently reveal painting attached either to surviving walls or fallen from the walls as the house decayed, and lying in layers on the ground. The lifting and reconstruction of such paintings is no light task and new techniques have had to be invented to solve this problem. The work is forging ahead in several countries, and the results can now be studied by art historians. At first research tended to be confined to the material known in each country with wall paintings found in Italy as the only comparative material available.

It soon became apparent that the student working on provincial material should be seeking the answer to several questions. First, the development of Roman wall painting in each particular province. Does it reflect particular trends in the choice of motifs? Secondly, how far does it resemble material found in other provinces? And thirdly, to what extent can these motifs be traced back to Italy, and how long was taken for their diffusion?

To assist in the solution of the second problem it was decided to hold a seminar on Provincial Wall Painting in Cambridge in 1980, and the topics discussed on that occasion are expanded in some of the papers in this volume. To them has been added the major account of current work on the Style II paintings from the Italian site of Settefinestre. This paper, together with Professor Peters' work on the Domus Aurea, provides material for answers to our third question. Another seminar is to be held in Paris in 1982.

The publication of this volume has been delayed by the editor's illness, and special thanks are due to Mrs. Diane Quarrie who undertook much extra work in addition to typing the manuscript.

Cambridge
1982

NOTE

1. *Journ. Brit. Arch. Ass.* IV.361.

List of Contributors

C. ALLAG., C.N.R.S., Centre d'étude des peintures murales romaines, Paris.

A. BARBET, C.N.R.S., Centre d'étude des peintures murales romaines, Paris.

E. FENTRESS, Rome.

LT-COL. G.E. GRAY, Priest's House Museum, Wimborne Minster.

DR.B. HEYWOOD, York Minster Archaeology Office.

DR.D.E. JOHNSTON, Dept. of Extra-Mural Studies, Southampton University.

DR.R. LING, Dept. of History of Art, Manchester University.

J. MELLOR, Leicester Museum.

DR. P. MEYBOOM, Amsterdam University.

DR. E. MOORMANN, Katholieke Universiteit, Nijmegen.

PROFESSOR W.J.Th. PETERS, Katholieke Universiteit, Nijmegen.

E. PYE, London University Institute of Archaeology.

DR. M. SCHLEIERMACHER, Römisch-Germanische Museum, Cologne.

DR. L.J.F. SWINKELS, Katholieke Universiteit, Nijmegen.

M. DE VOS, Rome

F. WEATHERHEAD, Cambridge.

1. A PAINTED OECUS FROM SETTEFINESTRE (TUSCANY) : EXCAVATION, CONSERVATION AND ANALYSES

Mariette de Vos, Fulvia Donati, Elizabeth Fentress,
Rossella Filippi, Cristina Panerai,
Maria Letizia Paoletti and Elizabeth Pye [1]

Introduction

From 1976 to 1981 a large six-week excavation has been undertaken every year at the Late Republican Roman villa of Settefinestre[2]. This excavation, jointly directed by Andrea Carandini and Tim Tatton-Brown, is a research and training excavation which has produced from the first very large quantities of painted wall plaster, and it has been an important aim to modify and improve techniques of recovering and restoring this material. This paper is a preliminary presentation of the methodology and results of the excavation and restoration of one room of the villa.[3]

The various processes which a decorative element undergoes before being published and placed in a museum or on a site are generally completely separated from one another. At best, excavation, conservation, restoration, analysis and art historical treatment are entrusted to different specialists, with the consequent loss of the information which might derive from a more organic treatment. At worst, the objects themselves finish up on the spoil heap. There are very few examples of Roman wall painting preserved in Italy outside the area of Vesuvius. The conservation of wall paintings is a long, delicate and expensive business, rarely foreseen when planning an excavation. One possibly way to overcome these problems is the formation of a research group which carries out the work from beginning to end, and in which the various specialists coordinate the whole process. This has been the case with the paintings from room 12, a small *oecus* giving onto the peristyle at Settefinestre.[4]

1. Excavation (Elizabeth Fentress)

While a certain amount has been written on the conservation of painted plaster little exists on its excavation.[5] Sites in which Roman painted plaster may be found *in situ* are rare indeed: normally the archaeologist is faced with a mass of fragments without any apparent relationship between them. This appeared to be the case at Settefinestre.

The principal structures of the villa - the *pars urbana* and the *pars rustica* - were constructed on a terrace supported by vaulted basements (*basis villae*). The level surface of the site has thus suffered little erosion. Further, the site has been devoted to olive

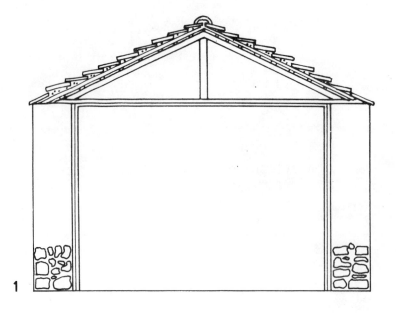

1.   The house

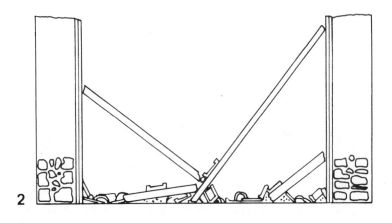

2.   The roof falls in.

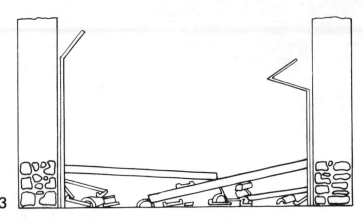

3.   Rain and frost detach the
     plaster from the walls.

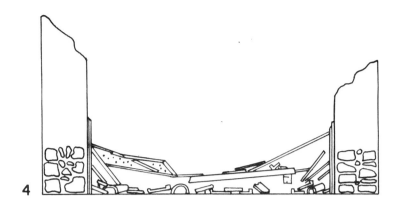

4. The walls collapse covering
   the fallen plaster but with
   plaster probably from adjacent
   rooms on top.

5. The resulting stratigraphy.

Fig.1.1. The formation of a destruction deposit.

cultivation, with the result that damage to the destruction layer has
been only slight, except in the immediate vicinity of the trees. They
are thus remarkably well preserved, with fallen stuccoed columns found
under as little as 20 cm. of topsoil.

In most of the *pars urbana* the upper destruction layer is marked
by the presence of numerous fragments of painted plaster. Their apparently
random distribution suggested at first a systematic collection, so as to
record at least the position of the fragments within a room. We thus
began the excavation of the small *oecus*, room 12, by constructing a
1 metre grid over the area of the room. Each individual grid square was
to be excavated in ten centimetre spits, the fragments of plaster from
each to be placed in boxes labelled with the grid square and spit number.
It was immediately obvious, however, that this system suffered from all
the usual defects of this type of excavation. Instead of revealing the
relationships between individual fragments it seemed to distort them.
Just as points of interest are inevitably situated at the junction of
two maps, so joining fragments rarely fell within one grid square. A
large quantity of individual fragments lay between two grid squares,
or, diagonally, between two spits. In sum, the system was revealed as
tedious, bureaucratic and counter-productive, and was abandoned almost
immediately. The experiment had at least demonstrated that fragments
of plaster had not fallen from the walls one by one, without any
recoverable relationship between them. Accurate trowelling revealed
large sheets of plaster, which had smashed on hitting the ground. The
collapse of the walls had given rise to a rather complicated stratigraphic sequence in which, within the layers, the units are spreads of
plaster, generally lying face down. The formation of this sequence
is summarized in Fig.1.1 as follows:

1. Schematic drawing of a room in the villa, shown in section. Over
a stone plinth some 60 cm. high the walls were constructed in *pisé de
terre*. 2. The roof falls in, probably due to the rotting of the beams[6]
3. Rain and frost detach the plaster from the walls. 4. The walls
themselves collapse, covering the layers of fallen plaster and filling
the interstices between the fragments. We have regularly found a
certain quantity of plaster lying face-up above the layer of clay
deriving from the walls, which seems to suggest that some plaster
continued to adhere to the walls as they collapsed, and was carried
with them into an adjoining room. 5. The resulting stratigraphy. It
should be noticed that the clay layer is deepest at the centre of the
room, as the plaster tends to accumulate around the walls.

For the recovery of the plaster we have adopted the following
procedure. First, individual spreads of plaster are revealed and cleaned
by careful trowelling (Pl.1.1). The highest spread - or that not covered
by any other - is planned at 1 to 20 on transparent drawing film
(Pl.1.3) and given a number. Beginning from one edge of the spread, the
fragments are collected in boxes lined with paper, taking care to preserve
the relationship between individual pieces (Pl.1.4). In very fractured
spreads the plaster is backed prior to lifting, (three to four coats of
a 3% solution of Paraloid B72 - an ethylacrylate/methyl methacrylate
copolymer - in acetone are applied together with a cotton gauze support).
Once filled, the box is numbered with the number of the spread and a
box number, as well as the usual site and layer information (Pl.1.2).
The area from which the box was taken is then outlined in red on the
plan, and the box number recorded (Fig. 1.2). Any fragments without a

Plate 1.1. Plaster spreads revealed by trowelling.

Plate 1.2. Box labelled with site, year, trench, room, layer, group and box number.

Plate 1.3. Grid square used for drawing plaster groups.   Plate 1.4. Plaster placed in boxes, showing position of fragments

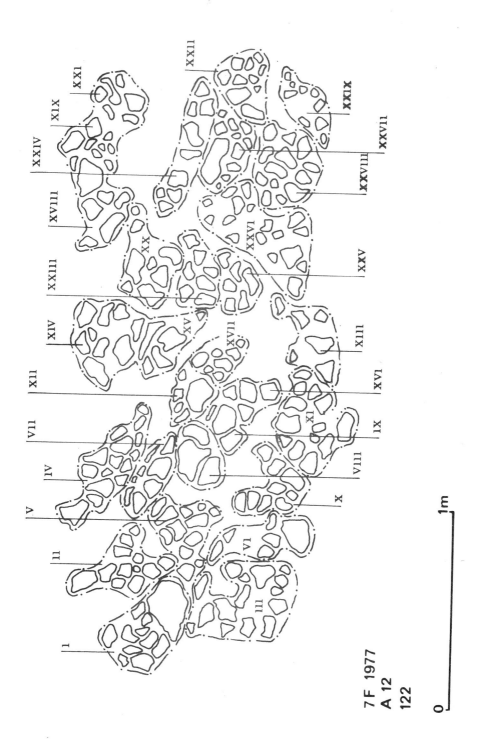

7 F 1977
A 12
122

0 ⊢————————⊣ 1m

Fig.1.2. Plan of spread of fallen plaster. Box numbers marked in
Roman numerals

clear relationship to a spread are collected in a box labelled with the
number of the nearest spread and marked 'sporadics'. Gaps between pieces
of plaster within a box are then filled with paper, and the whole is
tightly covered with mosquito netting held down with drawing pins.
Finally, the characteristics of each spread are recorded as follows:

SITE	YEAR	TRENCH	LAYER			
GROUP NO.	NO. OF BOXES	SPORADICS	POSITION PAINTED SURFACE	COVERED BY	COVERS	WALL(?)

This system has the advantage of a large degree of flexibility.
A spread may consist of a group of pieces small enough to fit into a
single box, or may extend to several square metres. When, as in the
1980 excavation, we have encountered less consistent falls of plaster
in which the groups are recoverable only as small nuclei, we have
retained the system with the slight modification that the area of the
group is defined on the plan but the individual nuclei are not drawn.
On the whole, however, it has been possible to recover the vast majority
of the plaster in a room within the context of a well-defined spread.

2. Reconstruction and Conservation (Cristina Panerai)

Reconstruction of the painting begins with the selection, guided
by the site plans, of one of the boxes.[7] The contents of this and each
succeeding box are cleaned, joined and recorded as as to become a piece
of the larger 'jig-saw puzzle' of the painting. During the processing
of each box a certain quantity of information about the painting is
destroyed, particularly the details of its preparation. It is therefore
necessary to record, box by box, the composition, thickness and type
of each layer of preparation, as well as any evidence for the construction of the walls and their treatment prior to painting. When necessary,
the evidence is drawn and photographed. As work progresses on each box,
the record sheet listing details of the preparation layers is also
used to record the condition of the painted surfaces, the type of
fracture between the plaster layers, the nature of any surface encrusta-
tions and any joins which can be made to the contents of other boxes.

Before removing the fragments of plaster from a box their edges
are traced on the paper lining the box to record their exact position
as found. The lower layers of plaster are then removed, usually by
pressure with a scalpel on the fracture lines, but in particularly
difficult cases with the use of a rotary sander.[8] The individual
fragment is marked on the back with the room number, layer, group and
box number, as well as with an individual number corresponding to its
position on the tracing. The plaster from room 12 was covered with a
large amount of clayey earth, easily removed with a dry brush. A soft
brush was used for the surface of the painting and a stiff one for the

edges, where eventual joins would be hindered by any dirt left in the cracks. Under the superficial layer of earth the paint surface was covered with a tenacious siliceous incrustation, on which various chemical preparations had little or no effect.[9] In the end we decided to resign outselves to exclusively mechanical cleaning with scalpels. This method is carried out working from the edge towards the centre, taking particular care with the overpainting which tends to adhere to the incrustation and come off with it.

When all the fragments in a box were cleaned it was possible to proceed to the more satisfying process of reassembling the fragments using the traced plan on the bottom of the box as a guide. Joins were marked with a chalked line. As each box was finished joins were stuck together with polyvinyl acetate solution adhesives such as UHU in order to form pieces about 20 centimetres square, no larger than can be held easily in one hand. The reassembled fragments from the finished box were left on a large table, and the next box begun - preferably that adjoining the first on the site plan. When the whole group was completed a search was made among the 'sporadics' for missing pieces: ideally these should be cleaned first and sorted according to colour and motif.

The work to date on room 12 has allowed an almost complete reconstruction of the decorative scheme. We have reassembled some two-thirds of the east wall (around 6 m^2),[10] half of the short north wall (Figs. 1.3,4) and a part of the west wall. There remains some yellowish plaster with traces of a reed backing (*camera a canne*), apparently from the ceiling, and a small group of fragments, around 50 x 70 cm., which appears to be of a different quality to the rest, and probably belongs to the architrave over the door on the south side. No more than two boxes of 'sporadic' fragments are left over.

The graphic documentation of the above includes a 1 to 1 drawing on plastic film and a 1 to 5 scale drawing with a minimum of reconstruction of the original design.

3. Conservation: The Support (Fulvia Donati)

The final operation on the painted plaster from room 12 was the mounting on a rigid support of the two relatively complete walls. The impetus for this undertaking was the exhibition based on the excavations at Settefinestre which opened in December 1978 at Pisa. The short time allowed for the preparation of this first exhibition led us to adopt a temporary solution for the mounting, in which in effect the fresco was stuck to two pieces of canvas nailed onto a wooden backing, and the whole made good with a plaster skim around the painting. The next year this temporary mounting, which had in the meantime buckled slightly, was replaced by a final version, constructed with the so-called 'sandwich' technique. This, while producing a reasonably successful result, retained certain of the inconveniences of the original mounting, principally the excessive weight of the reconstructed panel and the consequent tendency towards deformation of the wooden backing. Our third solution - that adopted for the mounting of the short wall, seems superior both for its lightness and for its greater simplicity (Fig.1.5). The support is constructed directly on the back

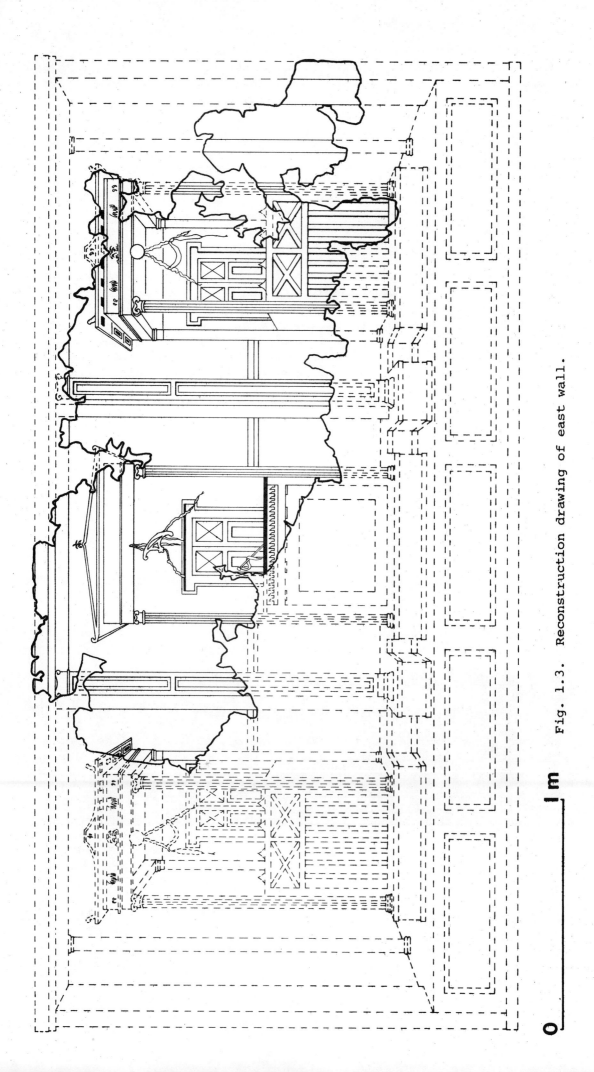

Fig. 1.3. Reconstruction drawing of east wall.

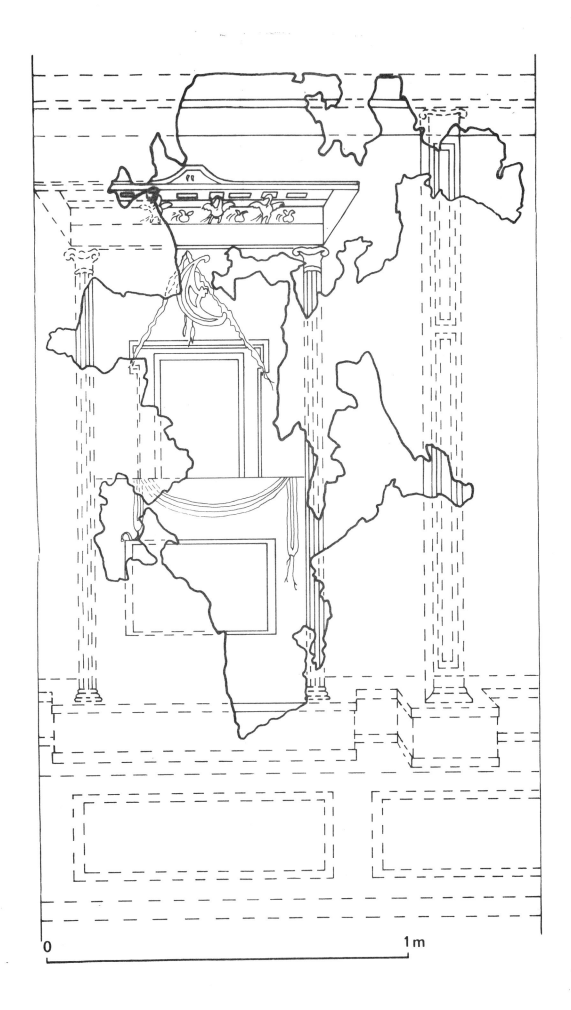

Fig. 1.4. Reconstruction drawing of north wall.

1 ALUMINIUM ANGLES

2 HONEYCOMB

3 GLASS FIBRE

4 MORTAR

5 FRESCO, MORTAR INFILL

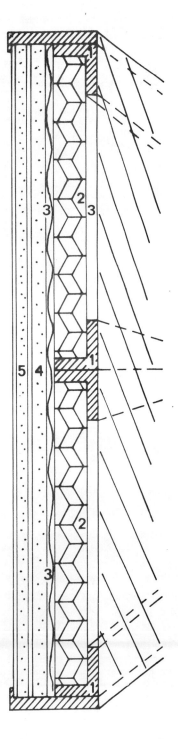

Fig. 1.5. The mounting of the reconstructed north wall.

of the fresco, which is laid on a sheet of polystyrene foam hollowed out to receive it. The whole is then covered with a second sheet and turned over. The process involves:

1.   The application to the back of the fresco and to the polystyrene of a synthetic mortar: 3 parts Movilith D.50, 1 part Movilith D.25, 1 part marble powder, 4 parts water (both Moviliths are polyvinyl acetate emulsions).

2.   On top of this mortar, while it is still wet, are placed a layer of glass fibre, then a sheet of plastic-impregnated cardboard 'honey-comb' and a second layer of glass fibre, all stuck together with ordinary Araldite (epoxy resin).

3.   T-section aluminium bars are inserted between the honeycomb and the glass fibre, both along the sides and to form an X across the back.

4.   The whole is then turned over and the surface made good, to just below the level of the painting, with lime plaster. Small lacunae are filled with a minimum of toned infill. A protective coating of 2-3% Paraloid B72 (an ethyl acrylate/methyl methacrylate copolymer) in trichloroethane is given to the painting.

We have decided against any restoration of the finished panel, neither incising nor colouring outside the limits of the fresco itself. The water-colour toning-in of *lacunae* has been as discreet as possible, as we feel that the picture should emerge by itself from the background of rough plaster.

4.   The Removal of the Dado (Elizabeth Pye)

Although most of the plaster had fallen with the *pisé de terre* and lay in fragments in the room, the dado remained attached to the stone footings of the walls and had to be removed in a different manner (Pl.1.1). As it had not been possible to remove the dado during the same season as the plaster fragments, the footings and plaster had been covered by a layer of plastic mosquito netting and carefully reburied. They were then re-excavated and the dado removed during the 1979 excavation season. All the work described below took place on the site or in. a temporary laboratory established in a local school.[11]

The limitations imposed by locally obtainable supplies (those brought out to the excavation were already exhausted) and the need for speed meant that normal methods were modified; only one layer of facing was used to remove the plaster, together with a locally obtained adhesive. Previous experience had however shown that the method worked well. A length of fine white cotton cloth was selected, the selvedges were cut off and the edges frayed to prevent marking of the plaster surface or undue tension when attaching the facing.

The cloth was thoroughly washed, using a non-ionic detergent (Synperonic N), to remove dressing and to pre-shrink, and then dried. A polyvinyl acetate emulsion (Vinavil 59) was chosen as the adhesive both because of its ease of use and its local availability in large quantities.[12]

The surface of the dado was prepared by brushing gently to remove

loose dust, earth and encrustation; roots and overhanging lumps of earth were cut away. Any fragments of plaster which had become detached or were embedded in the earthy deposits associated with the wall were carefully removed and placed in appropriately labelled bags. Once the remains of the dado had been cleaned it was possible to see the positions of the main fractures and therefore to decide how to divide the plaster into sections of a suitable size for lifting and removal. A plan was then made of the walls and the intended sections were measured and drawn in. A first coat of adhesive (diluted with an equal quantity of water) was brushed onto the plaster and the facing carefully applied to the now sticky surface, a second coat was then applied and, using the adhesive brush, the facing was manipulated into all hollows and round all projections so that it was properly in contact over the whole surface. Wherever a very deep hollow prevented complete adherence the facing was slit, gently pushed into the hollow and a patch applied over the area, and wherever more than one length of facing was needed the frayed edges were generously overlapped. (Pl.1.5).

Once the adhesive was dry, the facing was cut (using a scalpel) following the cracks already chosen as 'dividing lines' and each section was clearly numbered and arrowed, to indicate the right way up, on the loose area of facing left projecting at top and bottom. It was now possible to start detaching the plaster sections from the wall. Experience in other rooms on the site had shown that debris from the collapsing *pisé de terre* had often accumulated between the plaster and the stone wall-footings providing a useful cleavage line when removing such plaster dadoes. However, the plaster usually remained well attached at the base of the wall where a narrow but considerably thicker band of preparation was normally found associated with the second-style plaster work (Fig.1.6). Using hammer and chisels, a horizontal cut was first made along the base of the wall in order to free the plaster at this point, then, section by section, using long chisels and scalpels, the plaster was gradually worked away from the wall, detached and laid face downwards on prepared supporting boards (Pls. 1.6,7). Where necessary the board was held against the wall and plaster section and board gently lowered to the ground together. Fallen fragments which had been trapped behind the dado were collected and placed in labelled bags.

The sections were then brought back to the temporary laboratory and work started on cleaning and consolidation. With the plaster lying face downwards on the supporting boards, the back was cleaned of loose earth and roots (Pl.1.8). Three main methods were then used to consolidate the back of the plaster: very thin, broken and fragile fragments were given a continuous backing of a proprietary plaster and cellulose filler (Polyfilla); weak fragments were consolidated with a 5-10% solution in acetone of an ethyl acrylate/methyl methacrylate copolymer (Paraloid B72); large continuous areas with fine hairline cracks were temporarily backed with a thin cotton cloth and 20% solution of Paraloid B72 in acetone.[13] When fully consolidated from the back, each section could be turned over and the facing removed (Pl.1.9). The facing adhesive was partially dissolved using either acetone or, preferably, 95% ethyl alcohol (with a very little distilled water added).[14] A small area of the facing was wetted with the solvent at a time and, as the adhesive softened, the facing was gently rolled away holding a scalpel or spatula on the surface of the plaster to minimise danger of the cloth's catching and pulling fragments away in fragile areas (Pl.1.10).

Plate 1.6. A section of faced wallplaster being removed using a
           supporting board.

Plate 1.7. Sections of plaster lying face down on rigid supports.

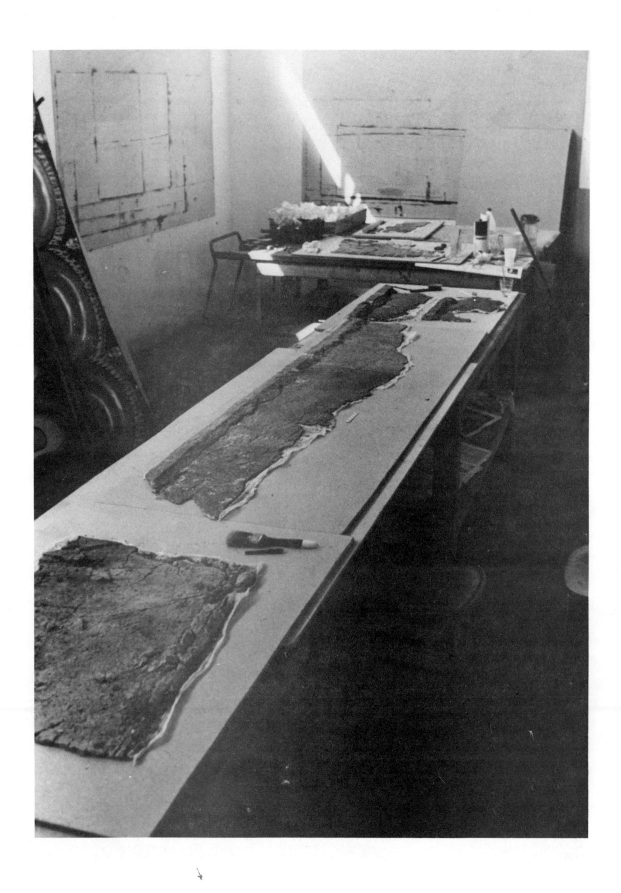

Plate 1.8.   The temporary laboratory showing plaster after cleaning of the back.

Plate 1.9. The longest section of plaster, face upwards, after
applying a temporary cloth backing.

Plate 1.10. The removal of the facing prior to cleaning the painted surface.

The largest continuous length of plaster was considerably buckled as a result of the collapse of the walls and it was decided to flatten it. After cleaning therefore the back of the plaster was fairly liberally wetted with acetone to soften the facing adhesive; distorted areas were gently pressed downwards and kept weighed down while the acetone evaporated and the facing adhesive re-hardened. The back was then reinforced with cotton cloth and a 20% solution of Paraloid B72 in acetone.

After removal of the facing, a preliminary cleaning was undertaken on the surface to remove both the remains of the adhesive and the heavy silicate encrustation over the paint layer. This involved the careful use of surgical scalpels and of cotton wool swabs slightly moistened in distilled water (with a few drops of non-ionic detergent added) rolled over the surface. It is hoped that after final cleaning it will be possible to marry up the dado to the already reconstructed walls.

5. The Fresco : Technique (Rosella Filippi)

The *pisé de terre* walls at Settefinestre appear to have been scored before applying the plaster, to facilitate the adhesion of the preparation layers. Similarly, the snail pointing of the stone foundation shows pick-axe marks, apparently carried out for the same purpose.

Thin section analysis carried out on six samples of the plaster revealed that it was composed of five layers. These comprised, in order of application (Fig.1.6):

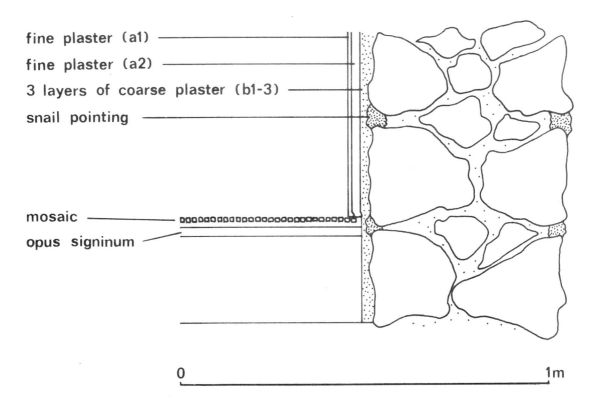

fine plaster (a1)

fine plaster (a2)

3 layers of coarse plaster (b1-3)

snail pointing

mosaic

opus signinum

0   1m

Fig. 1.6. Section of wall and pavement.

21

1. B 1-3. Three layers of coarse pale grey plaster, consisting of
lime and river sand, with occasional fragments of tile. The grain si
was extremely variable, with an average diameter of 4 mm. The total
thickness of these three layers varied from thirty five to sixty mm.,
while the individual layers varied as follows: B 1/13-18 mm., B 2/
21-25 mm., B 3/5-30 mm. It is clear that much of the variation is due
to B 3, which represents the initial levelling coat.

2. A 2. A layer of white plaster some 9 mm. thick, composed of homogeneous lime and fine calcite (ca. 2 mm.), whose uniform dimensions
suggest sieving.

3. A 1. The layer to which the paint was applied. This was ca. 1 mm.
thick, consisting of lime and very fine calcite. The uppermost part
contained minute fragments of tourmaline, oriented parallel to the
surface, which suggests that a final smoothing was given to the
surface before the paint was applied.

The neighbourhood of the villa was probably the source of all the
materials used; the sand was presumably derived from the Albegna river,
while deposits of tourmaline are present on the island of Giglio.

The five successive applications of plaster seen here may be
compared with the recommendations of Vitruvius. He recommends seven
applications, of which the last three should contain lime and ground,
sieved calcite (VII,3,6). Neither of these procedures was consistently
followed for the preparation of painted wall plaster, however; the
majority of the plaster at Pompeii consists of only two or three layers,
while the rather expensive calcite was often substituted by sand. The
presence at Settefinestre of calcite as well as five successive
applications of plaster indicates the relatively high quality of the
workmanship.

6.   The Decoration (Mariette de Vos)

All the decorative elements of the villa are recorded on the
record sheet presented here (Figs.1.7,8).[15] This particular sheet is
designed to be used on the three main components of a room's decoration - pavement, walls and ceiling, as well as for decorative elements
found in the course of the excavation such as stuccoed cornices or
columns.

The bringing together of all the decorative elements in a room
into a single record sheet has been carried out less for practical and
economic reasons than for the necessity to consider them as a single
aspect of the building. This works against the tendency to concentrate
on one class of material or a single aspect (technique, conservation,
iconography, stylistic variation etc.) and thereby to obscure the
relationship between architectural form and its decoration, with the
consequent loss of the social, psychological and functional connotations
of the whole.[16] Only from an analytic catalogue can one get a
comprehensive view of the decoration.

Examination of the relationship between the pavement and the wall
in room 12 (Fig.1.6) reveals a characteristic common to all rooms of

the first phase of the villa: the primary layers (No.3 in B 1-3) of preparation continue 13 cm. below the level of the pavement. The two upper layers (A 1 and 2) cover the margin of the mosaic. These two layers are keyed together immediately above the level of the mosaic.[17] The mosaic in room 12 is preserved only along the edges, where it was protected by the wall plaster. The rest was robbed in antiquity. Here it is composed of white *tesserae* running obliquely to the axis of the room. This is the case in all the other mosaics from the first phase of the villa. A more or less square depression in the preparation at the centre of the room suggests the presence of an *emblema*, placed at the intersection of the axes of the architectural motives on the walls. The ideal viewpoint for the walls remains the entrance to the room from the peristyle.

The decorative scheme of the side walls is a tri-partite stage setting in the tradition of the Pompeian second style. It represents three *aediculae* with architrave and projecting lintel. The central building is separated from the viewer by a screen with a dentillated cornice, those on the side with gates topped with a row of spikes (*aculei*). These structures are painted on a blue ground suggesting the sky, and are situated in a portico with dark pink pilasters, possibly intended to be wooden. The end wall is also tripartite in form. The single *aedicula* preserved (Fig.1.4) has a lintel with modillions, supported by swans. Hanging at the centre are a pelta and garlands, while on the screen blocking the door there appears to be a *pinax,* if this is not a window in the screen. The area between this structure and the plinth is missing, probably because it coincides with the break between the stone foundations of the wall and the part in *pisé de terre*, and was thereby liable to shatter. This would probably have shown a podium with project- ing wings.

The light in the painting is keyed to the natural light-source of the room, its entrance onto the peristyle. The herring-bone perspective is not very accurate. There are no exact parallels for this scheme but the closest seems to be the Room of the Masks in the House of Augustus on the Palatine (36-28 B.C., last period of the second style).[18] The design of three *aediculae* on each wall is uncommon, but when found at Rome or in the Vesuvian centres it is among the richest decorations. Settefinestre provides one of the few examples of second-style decora- tion north of Rome apart from the complexes of Bolsena (Barbet 1971: 332-388), Ancona (*EAA* 1970:57- Brescia, (Mirabella Roberti 1963:251- 253) and Glanum (Barbet 1974:11).

We are less well-informed on the ceiling. The small panel painted to represent coffers in perspective, which appears to have come from the architrave, suggests that the original ceiling may also have been painted with coffers, if indeed it was not carried out in stucco. The yellowish plaster previously mentioned is clearly derived from the ceiling, but its poor quality contrasts with the wall plaster. Stucco cornices are completely lacking, although they are found in a number of other rooms around the peristyle, as in general in late republican decoration, where they underline the architectonic articulation (Vitruvius VII 3, 1-4; Van Buren 1924:112-122). The absence of these in room 12 may be explained if one suggests that the reeds supporting the ceiling would have been more liable to rot than the rest of the structure, and that the collapse of the ceiling would have brought down the stuccoes. The ceiling would then have been restored without stuccoes

LOCATION	YEAR	TRENCH	ROOM	DECORATIVE STRATI-GRAPHIC UNIT IN SITU AND/OR RECONSTRUCTED
PLANS	SECTIONS	ELEVATIONS	PHOTOGRAPHS	

DEFINITION AND COLLOCATION

TECHNIQUE OF FACING	MATERIAL(S)

PHYSICAL SEQUENCE	IDENTICAL TO		JOINED TO		STRATIGRAPHIC SEQUENCE (MATRIX)	ABOVE
	BUTTED BY		BUTTS			BELOW
	COVERED BY		COVERING			

PREPARATION OF THE BACKING	LAYER	1⁰	2⁰	3⁰	4⁰
	THICKNESS MM MIN MAX				
	INORGANIC COMPONENTS (sand, lime, calcite, pozzo-lana, grog, other)				
	ORGANIC COMPONENTS (straw, reeds, other)				
	SINOPIA IMPRESSED STRING GRAFFITO				
	REVERSE impression				

FACING (plain, brush marks, other)				

COLOURS

SUPERIMPOSITION OF COLOUR LAYERS

OTHER

DECORATIVE SCHEME

PROFILES

Fig. 1.7. Recording sheet for elements of architectural decoration.

MOSAIC, OPUS SECTILE		COLOURS			
		MATERIALS (stone, vitreous, ceramic)			
		FORM (surface)			
		DIMENSIONS min max med HEIGHT			
	tes-serae	No per 100 CM²			
		WEAVE			

RELATIONSHIP BETWEEN ARCHITECTURE AND DECORATION

DATING ELEMENTS

DATING

PERIOD	STYLE	PHASE

BIBLIOGRAPHY

PARALLELS

STATE OF PRESERVATION	SUPERFICIAL DEPOSITS		HEAVY INCRUSTATIONS
	DEGREE OF ADHESION		DEGREE OF COHESION
	GAPS		
	SIGNS OF WEAR		
	OTHER		

CONSERVATION TREATMENT	CONSOLIDATION	ADHESIVE
	FABRIC FACING	DETACHING
	PACKING	TEMPORARY COVERING
	SAMPLE(S) FOR ANALYSIS	LABORATORY LOCATION
DATE		SUPERVISOR

Fig.1.8. Recording sheet (reverse).

or painting.

This decorative scheme, probably dating from early in the second half of the first century B.C., is interesting when placed on conjunction with other decorative elements from the villa such as the *scutulatum* in *opus sectile* from the 'Corinthian' *oecus* or the profile of the *tufo impluvium* (a *cyma* between two *tori*). If these elements had been found on their own the suggested dating might have been considerably earlier.[19] As it is, they suggest a conservative element in the decoration of the villa.

7. The Iconographic Scheme (M. Letizia Paoletti)

The iconography of the scene represented on the walls of the *oecus* appears to have its origins in the theatre. The wooden pilasters in the foreground rest on a podium, while the middle distance is occupied by three *aediculae*, with gates painted to suggest their wooden construction (Figs. 1.3,4). The tripartite scheme of the walls recalls an essential feature of ancient theatre, the arrangement of the *scaenae frons* into three doors, representing the three houses of the central characters of the play.[20] *Aediculae* were used as temporary architectural features on the stage. Their architectural framework and their decorative elements (garlands, ribbons, shields, etc.) can be close paralleled with those depicted on the Apulian vases of the IVth century B.C. These, and the *paraskenia*, or wings projecting from the stage, are said to have been introduced into the Roman tradition of temporary wooden theatre from Apulia by Livius Andronicus, Ennius and Pacuvius, who were among the first transmitters of Greek culture to the Latin world. *Aediculae* continued in the Latin theatre under the major comedians Plautus and Terence, as can be inferred from *Asinaria* 424 f. and *Amphitryo* 1008 f. In the form represented here the architectural design consisted of two or more columns framing a doorway, and supporting a roof, (Fig.1.9).

The suggestion that the decoration of this room is derived from theatre design seems to be supported by a passage from Vitruvius (VII, 5, 1, 2) which mentions *scaenarum frontes* among decorative subjects for wall paintings.[21] The use of these motives provided the opportunity to suggest illusionistic space, thereby increasing the apparent size of the room. Further, the reference to the architectural treatment of public spaces underlined the luxurious nature of the private house in which the paintings were executed.

NOTES

1. Elizabeth Fentress translated this paper; Mariette de Vos, Elizabeth Fentress and Elizabeth Pye prepared it for publication. Jason Wood undertook the redrawing of the figures.

2. The excavation is supported by both an Italian and a British Committee and financed by the Regione Toscana, the Consiglio Nazionale delle Ricerche, the University of Pisa, the British Academy, the Gordon Childe Fund of the University of London

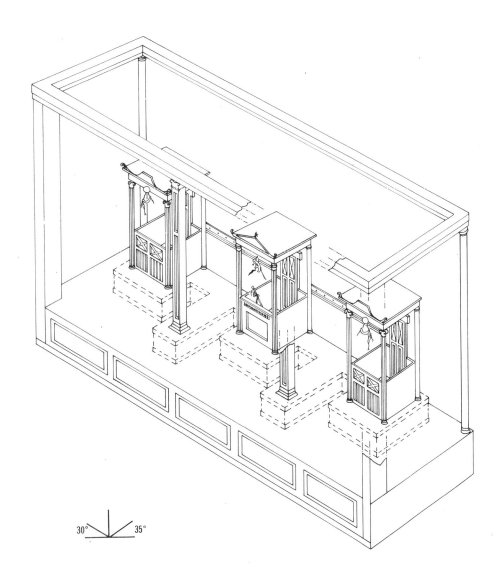

Fig.1.9. Isometric reconstruction of the stage represented on the east wall.

Institute of Archaeology, the Cotton Foundation, the Craven Fund
of the University of Oxford, the Faculty of Classics of the
University of Cambridge, the Society of Antiquaries of London and
the Trustees of the British Museum. A full interim report on the
excavation was published in the summer of 1979 (A.Carandini and
S.Settis, 1979) in conjunction with a special exhibition coordinated by S.Settis, which has been shown in many towns in Italy, as
well as in England and France since December 1978.

3. An interim report was also produced in *Roman Villas in Italy,
   recent excavations and research* (British Museum, Occasional Paper,
   No.24, 1980 ed. K. Painter pp.9-22).

4. The excavation of the wallplaster from room 12 was supervised by
   Elizabeth Fentress, and she was responsible for the excavation
   technique described below, helped by Fulvia Donati, who has coordinated the Italian conservation group consisting of Rossella
   Filippi, Cristina Panerai and Letizia Paoletti, the result of
   whose work has been the restoration of this room. Stylistic
   analysis of the decoration of the villa has been undertaken by
   Mariette de Vos. The British Conservation team consisted of
   Elizabeth Pye and students from the Conservation Department, the
   University of London Institute of Archaeology. Miss Pye was
   responsible for working out a method of detaching the wallplaster
   that still adhered to the bottom of the walls, and this is now
   also being undertaken by groups from Siena and Pisa. Since the
   summer of 1980 a group of restorers from the Istituto Centrale
   (Rome) has also participated in this work.

5. Barbet (1969) suggests excavation using a grid. Durante (1977:
   327,328) provides a phenomenology of plaster collapse, but does
   not discuss its excavation. Recently, R. Sabrie (1980) has
   published an article on excavation techniques with figures
   miraculously similar to our Figs. 1.1 and 1.2 (previously presented
   in the exhibition 'Schiavi e Padroni in Etruria Meridionale'
   Pisa-Rome 1978-79).

6. It is possible that a large proportion of the tiles were salvaged
   before the abandonment of the villa, as the number found in
   excavation never coincides with that required to cover a room.
   This might account for the fact that in one room a large sheet
   of plaster had fallen directly onto the pavement, before the fall
   of the remainder of the roof. Holes left in the roof by robbing
   had hastened the detachment of the wall plaster.

7. The conservation of the wall plaster took place in a laboratory in
   the Institute of Archaeology at Pisa, provided by the kind assist-
   ance of S. Settis and the director of the Institute, L. Beschi.
   The work of conservation was undertaken by numerous students at
   the Institute, among them I. Attolini, R. Camaiora, G. Lippi,
   L. Neri, G. Ricci and A. Vittori, as well as Linda Mitchell and
   John Olive of the London Institute of Archaeology. We are also
   grateful for the help of Pierluigi Campagni, secretary of the
   Institute. We benefitted greatly from a month spent in the labora-
   tory of A. Barbet at the Centre d'Étude des Peintures Murales
   Romaines at Soissons, and from the advice of P. and L. Mora and
   M. Picchi. The conservation of Roman wall painting is discussed

by Barbet, 1969 and n.d. No.2.

8. While Barbet (1969:78-79) suggests that the removal of the
    preparation layer should take place only during the last stages
    of reconstruction we found that an early removal was imposed by
    the difficulty of laying out adjoining pieces of unequal thick-
    ness without enormous sand trays. Further, removal after stick-
    ing the fragments together is almost impossible without rebreaking
    the joins. As long as any evidence for wall construction found on
    the preparation plaster is fully recorded before removal we see
    no reason why this should not take place immediately.

9. The pack suggested by P. and L. Mora (1972:4) had a certain
    effect on the incrustation, but tended to remove certain colours
    not resistant to water. A dentist's drill was also tried, but
    this proved risky and not particularly effective.

10. The rest of this wall appears to have fallen down into the stair-
    case leading to the *basis villa*.

11. The team consisted of Elizabeth Pye, Richard Jaeschke and Gillian
    Juleff.

12. Polyvinylacetate emulsion can be diluted with water, gives off
    no unpleasant or toxic solvent vapours, has good 'tack' and a
    relatively slow rate of drying. Vinavil 59 is used by Italian
    restorers who find it remains reversible over a considerable
    period of time.

13. Acetone was used in the absence of any other suitable solvent.
    There was, of course, a slight danger that the facing adhesive
    (polyvinyl acetate) might soften, but as long as the plaster
    remained face downwards, undisturbed and fully supported on a
    board there was no difficulty; once the acetone had fully
    evaporated the facing adhesive had again hardened.

14. Ethyl alcohol was used as it was the only alcohol obtainable
    locally. It was preferred because of its slower evaporation rate
    but it was considerably more expensive than acetone. Addition of
    water to the alcohol increases the working time but may overwet
    the plaster in the fragile areas. Therefore, where the plaster
    surface was exceptionally fragile either ethyl alcohol alone or
    acetone or a mixture of the two were used, and alcohol was always
    used to remove the facing from areas consolidated or backed with
    Paraloid B72.

15. Record sheet now used by the Istituto per il Catalogo e la
    Documentazione of the Ministero dei Beni Culturali e Ambientali.
    The staff of the Istituto Centrale del Restauro collaborated on
    the section recording conservation.

16. Corlaìta Scagliarini 1976, Clarke 1979; de Vos 1979; Joyce 1979.
    See also the rather theoretical structuralist analysis of Bruneau,
    1976.

17. A number of fragments of tile with herring-bone incisions and
    nail-locks which served for the adhesion of the plaster were found

at Settefinestre, but none was found *in situ*. At Pompeii there is only one example, a tile fixed in the doorpost in the Casa del Marinaio (VII 15, 2,d; Gaedechens 1872). Their use is attested in northern Italy at Bolsena, Rimini, (Zuffi 1964:73-4 and Fig. 20) and Trento (Tosi 1978:151).

18. Carettoni 1961; Beyen 1969. Another house at Pompeii is stylistically very close, if not of the same workshop (I, 6, 2-4, Casa del Criptoportico).

19. Carandini, Settis 1979 pl. 28. *Scutulatum* pavements carried out in *opus sectile* date from the second half of the 2nd century B.C. through to the first quarter of the first century B.C. At Pompeii there are two examples contemporary with the first phase of the second style: the Villa of Diomede and the House of Triptolemos (VII, 7, 5; de Vos 1979, 116 and n. 49). In Pompeii the impluvia in tufo are generally considered to be pre-sullan (Fadda 1975: 161-66).

20. On the construction of wooden stage sets Vitruvius V, 6, 3-8; Pliny *N. H.* XXXVI, 114; Tacitus *Ann.* XIV, 20; Pollux *Onomasticon* IV, 124 f.

21. The idea that theatre design influenced painting of the second style has been denied, most recently by Engemann (1967) and Picard (1977). However, it should be noted that all three doors on the paintings from Settefinestre are unique in being represented as such, and that the composition of the whole fits perfectly into what is known of the development of Roman theatre design.

BIBLIOGRAPHY

Barbet, A. n.d. *Bulletin de liaison du Centre d'Étude sur la Peinture Murale Romaine* nos. 2 and 4.

Barbet, A. 1969 'La restauration des peintures murales d'époque romaine' *Gallia* 17 (1969) 71-92.

Barbet, A. 1971 'Peintures murales de deuxième style provenant de la terrasse Sud-Est, zone A, couche 3' *Fouilles de l'École Francaise de Rome a Bolsena (Poggio Moscini) II, les architectures Rome,* 321-388.

Barbet, A. 1974 'Recueil général des peintures murales de la Gaule' *Gallia* Sup. 27 (1974) 11-65.

Barbet, A and Allag, C. 1972 'Techniques de préparation des parois dans la peinture murale romaine' *MEFRA* 84 (1972) 935-1069.

Beyen, H. 'Die neuentdeckten Malereien auf den Palatin' *Bulletin Antieke Beschaving,* 39 (1964) 140-143).

Bruneau, P. 'La mosaique grecque classique et hellénistique' *Archeologia Warzawa* (1976) 38-42.

Carandini, A. and Settis, S.   1959   *Schiavi e padroni nell'Etruria meridionale*. Bari.

Carettoni, G.   1961   'I due nuovi ambienti dipinti sul Palatino' *Bollettino d'Arte* 46 (1961) 189-199.

Clarke, J.   1979   *Roman Black and White Figural Mosaics*.   New York.

Corlaìta Scagliarini, D.   1976   'Spazio e decorazione nella pittura pompeiana', *Palladio* 33-35 (1974-1976) 3-44.

de Vos, M.   1979a   'Pavimenti e mosaici', *Pompei 79*. Naples 1979, 161-176.

de Vos, M.   1979b   'Synopsis del repertorio ornamentale di pitture e pavimenti di terzo stile' in Bastet, F., de Vos, M., *Il terzo stile,* The Hague.

Durante, A.   1977   'Gli intonaci dipinti della domus orientale (Casa degli Affreschi)' in Frova, A., et al. *Scavi di Luni* II, Rome 1977:327-328 and Pl.V.

EAA: *Enciclopedia di arte antica, classica e orientale*. Supplemento 1970. Roma 1973.

Engemann, J.,   1967   'Architekturdarstellungen des fruhen zweiten Stils' *RM* Suppl. 12, Heidelberg.

Fadda, N.   1975   'Gli impluvi modanati delle case di Pompei' *Neue Forschungen in Pompeji* Recklinghausen 1975, 161-166.

Gaedechens, R.   1872   'Nuovi scavi di Pompei; la strada del gallo' *Bullettino dell'Istituto di Corrispondenza Archeologica* 1872, 161-177.

Joyce, H.   1979   'Form, function and technique in the pavements of Delos and Pompeii', *AJA* 83 (1979) 253-263.

Lanciani, R.   1871   'Recenti scoperti in Roma e nelle vicinanze' *Bullettino dell'Istituto de Corrispondenza Archeologica* 1871, 21-30.

Mirabella Roberti, M.   1963   *Storia de Brescia I* Brescia.

Mora, P.   1967.   'Proposte sulla tecnica della pittura murale romana' *Bullettino dell'Istituto Centrale del Restauro*, 1967, 63-84.

Mora, P., and L.   1977   'Problemi di Conservazione' in G. Urbani ed.: *Atti della Commissione per lo sviluppo tecnologico della Conservazione dei Beni Culturale*. Tome 1977:4-16.

Ricard, G.,   1977   'Peinture et théatre au Ier siècle avant J.-C.' *RA* (1977) 178-179.

Sabrié, R.   1980   'La fouille des enduits peints' *Peinture murale en Gaule, actes des séminaires*. Dijon 1980, 53-60.

Tosi, G.   'La casa romana di via A. Rosmini a Trento' *Aquileia nostra*
       49 (1978) 151-162.

Van Buren, A.   'The technique of stucco ceilings at Pompeii' *JRS* 14
       (1924) 112-122.

Zuffi, M.   1964   'Nuove scoperte di archeologica e storia riminese'
       Studi romagnoli 13 (1964) 73-74.

2. THE ROOTS OF PROVINCIAL ROMAN PAINTING
RESULTS OF CURRENT RESEARCH IN NERO'S DOMUS AUREA

W.J.Th. Peters
and
P.G.P. Meyboom

Students of provincial Roman wall-painting looking for parallels in Italy will inevitably come across Nero's Domus Aurea, or rather the pavilion of that enormous complex which is very largely preserved under the ruins of the baths of Trajan on the Colle Oppio in Rome. That is sufficient reason for us to draw attention to the research which we have been carrying out over the last few years into the paintings in that same building.[1]

It would have been logical to have postponed a study of the painting in the Domus Aurea until our Italian colleagues had completed their architectural research, which is being supported by new excavations.[2] However, the continuing deterioration of the paintings, in so far as they have been preserved, has now reached a critical phase which means that further postponement would be unjustifiable.

The most important excavations and some publications

The first extensive excavations in the Domus Aurea, which used to be called the baths of Titus, were carried out by the English architect Ch. Cameron who reported on them in his book *The Baths of the Romans, Les bains des Romains* of 1772.[3] In 1774 the Roman art dealer Ludovico Mirri partially excavated eleven rooms. He had a number of drawings of walls and vaults made and published them in the form of engravings with a text by Giuseppe Carletti in *Le antiche camere delle Terme di Tito e le loro pitture* of 1776.[4] Other excavations were conducted from 1811 to 1814 by A. de Romanis, who published his results in *Le antiche camere esquiline dette comunemente delle Terme di Tito* in 1822. In 1912, A. Muñoz and F. Weege began their excavations. The latter gave an account of the findings in his article 'Das Goldene Haus des Nero' in *Jahrbuch des Deutschen Archäologischen Instituts*, 28 (1913), 127-244. From 1931 onwards, with the odd interruption, excavations were carried out by the Soprintendenza Archeologica di Roma.[5] The recent literature on the Domus Aurea is very voluminous.[6] However, up to today there has been no single publication that has covered everything which is now available, either from the point of view of architecture or painting. For the study of the paintings, especially of those on the vaults, the book by Nicole Dacos, *La découverte de la Domus Aurea et la formation des grotesques a la renaissance* of 1969, is of great importance. This author also wrote 'Fabullus et l'autre peintre de la Domus Aurea' in *Dialoghi di archeologia*, 2 (1968), 210-226.

Building history and inhabitants

The building history of the pavilion in question, which we will refer to as Domus Aurea for the sake of convenience, is extremely

33

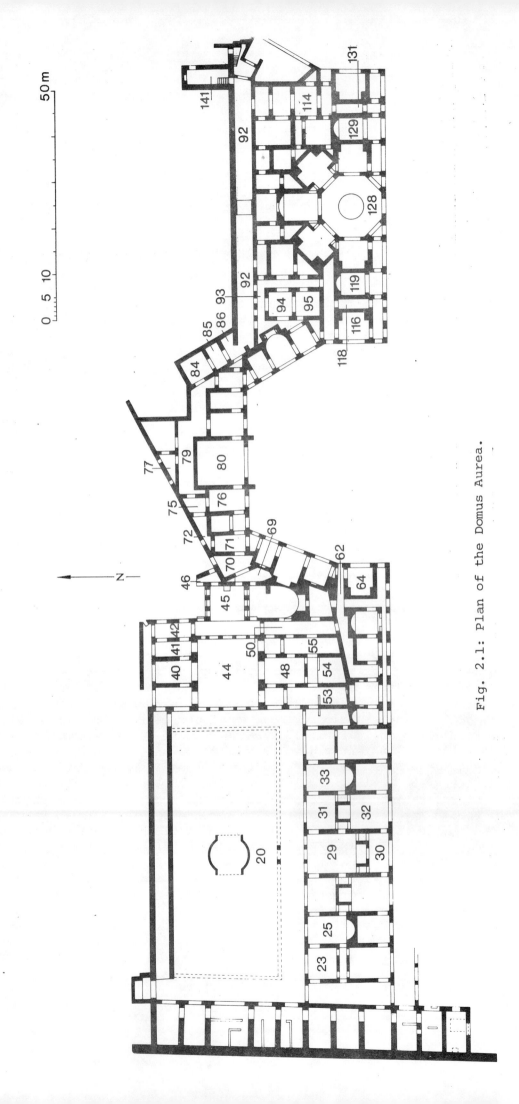

Fig. 2.1: Plan of the Domus Aurea.

complicated (fig. 2.1).[7] Building began after the Great Fire of Rome in 64 A.D. Parts of existing buildings were incorporated into the new building. Even during the building stage and before plaster and paint were applied, all kinds of changes were made. Throughways were reduced in size or blocked up, and windows were turned into niches or completely closed off.

In order to build the nymphaeum no.45, east of the peristyle no.20,[8] two rooms, nos. 46 and 69, whose walls had already been furnished with paintings had to be partially demolished. From this and from other indications in the same surroundings one can conclude that the nymphaeum and the rooms of the peristyle wing connected to it are more recent than the rooms leading directly onto the five-sided courtyard. Of the changes to the large exedra no. 44, between the peristyle no.20 and the open courtyard in front of the nymphaeum no.45, the alterations whereby the north and south walls were strengthened in order to carry a large barrel vault is of particular importance for dating the paintings in the neighbouring room no.48. Finally, there are clear traces of cores of non-imperial habitation, principally evident in the beam holes of the floors, by means of which upper storeys were built in the high rooms.

Occupation of the pavilion ended in 104 A.D. when those parts that could be used as such were made into a substructure of the baths of Trajan. To the east a section was demolished. The octagonal domed room no.128, which now lies off-centre, most probably originally lay on the axis of the building; there was certainly a second five-sided courtyard, and presumably the preserved peristyle had its counterpart to the east.[9] When the building fell into disuse, the costly material, such as the marble of the dados, was removed and the rooms were very largely filled with rubble, which still has not entirely been removed. The renaissance artists who made sketches of the paintings - which they called grotesques - at the end of the fifteenth century walked on top of the rubble and only saw the upper zones of the walls and vaults.[10]

Among the data available to us about the building history of the Domus Aurea and, consequently, about its wall-paintings there are a number of written sources. Within the framework of this paper, the following are important.

Tacitus (*Annals* XV, 39 and 42) and Suetonius (*De Vita Caesarum, VI, Nero,* 31) tell us that the Domus Transitoria burnt down in 64 A.D. and that the building of the Domus Aurea began subsequently.

Suetonius (*De Vita Caesarum, VII, Otho,* 7) states that Otho's first act as a ruler was to vote a sum of 'quingenties sestertium' (50,000,000 sesterces) for the completion of the Domus Aurea. However, we do not know whether this money was fully or partially used for its intended purpose during Otho's three months' reign. We can conclude that Otho regarded the Domus Aurea as the imperial dwelling but it should be noted that the pavilion that we know remained unfinished.

Nero's Domus Aurea, we read in Dio Cassius (*Historia Romana* 65, 4,2) could not satisfy Vitellius, and his wife Galeria ridiculed the meagre amounts of decoration found in the royal apartments. From this text one might deduce that the imperial family did not live in the Domus Aurea. However, one ought to allow for the possibility that, after actually moving in, Vitellius and Galeria did not find their stay in the as yet unfinished pavilion to their liking.

Pliny the Elder reports in his *Naturalis Historia* (XXXIV, 84) that Vespasian had the statues that Nero had erected in his Domus Aurea dedicated in the Temple of Peace. This fitted in perfectly with Vespasian's policy, for it was he who incidentally had the Amphitheatrum Flavium, known to us as the Colosseum, built on the very spot where the large central pond in Nero's town villa lay. We cannot expect this emperor to have completed an undertaking begun by Nero.

Pliny the Elder also writes in his *Naturalis Historia* (XXXVI, 37) that in his time the Laocoon group was to be found in Titus' house. As C.C. van Essen[11] has convincingly shown, this group was discovered in the year 1506 in the neighbourhood of Sette Sale, actually on the site of the Domus Aurea, but not in room no.129 (Weege no.80) of the preserved pavilion, as Weege[12] claimed. So one cannot use the extract from Pliny mentioned above as direct evidence that Titus occupied the pavilion in question.

The paintings

Most of the paintings of the Domus Aurea can be attributed to the phase of imperial occupation, and some to the non-imperial phase.

A number of rooms were not provided with paintings at all, either in the imperial phase or subsequently.

In many rooms where the paintings were indeed completed during the building phase, the dado was never faced with marble as had been planned and the wall remained unplastered. In a number of cases the zone reserved for the marble dado was plastered in a later phase, after which it was either decorated or left blank.

Generally speaking the paintings whose remnants are so few that one can say very little about their system, will not be included in this brief overview.

The paintings of the period of imperial occupation

Before we deal with the paintings of the period of imperial occupation of the Domus Aurea, we should bear in mind that, with the exception of the dome of the octagonal room no.128, the nymphaeum no.45 and the exedra no.44, which is situated in front of it, paintings were applied everywhere to the vaults, sometimes in combination with plaster relief-work; however the art on the walls took a subordinate role. The more important the room the higher the marble facing went in the original state. Thus in the central room of the west wing, no.29, to the south of the peristyle, the marble panelling reached to the point where the vaulting began, the wellknown 'volta delle civette'.[13]

According to Pliny the Elder (*Naturalis Historia* XXXV, 120), the Domus Aurea was the 'carcer', the prison, of the art of the painter Famulus (Fabullus),[14] and for this reason there were not many other examples of his work to be found. He spent only a few hours a day in painting and he always wore a toga, even on the scaffolding. Nicole Dacos[15] ascribes to him the more elaborate paintings accentuated by plaster relief, both on the walls and the vaults. He was very likely not involved in the mural painting systems and the rather simple vault decorations which will be discussed in this paper.

When studying the paintings of the imperial phase, we deal with

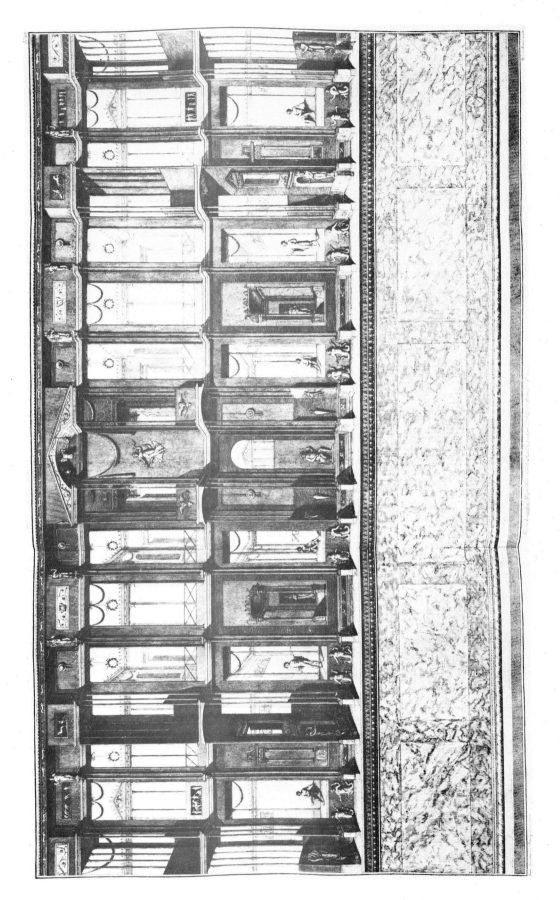

Plate 2.1:   Rome, Domus Aurea, room no. 50 (after Mirri and Carletti).

PLATE 2.2:   Rome, Domus Aurea, room no. 42, east wall
(Copyright Nijmegen University).

various systems which can be divided into two main groups:
a extremely elaborate ornamental facades which occupy the main and upper zones and which, with one exception, can be classified under 'scaenae frontes';
b walls whose middle zones in the main consist of fields or, on occasion, of simple scaenae frontes, combined with simple scaenae frontes or aediculae connected by linear patterns in one or more upper zones.

The first group of paintings is not of direct interest for the study of provincial-Roman painting, but within the general framework we cannot do without it, so we will deal with it briefly. The simpler paintings of the latter group do offer direct links with provincial art, and these will be dealt with more extensively.

Hypotactic ornamental facades or scaenae frontes

The elaborated scaenae frontes in the Domus Aurea divide into two groups:
a those with somewhat heavy architecture - albeit not abnormally so for the fourth style - which is polychrome on a white background, occasionally accentuated by means of plaster relief;
b those with very light architecture which is usually polychrome, sometimes oligochrome, and is always applied to a red or yellow background.

One example from each group will be dealt with. The most characteristic representatives from each of the two systems are unfortunately only known to us through the engravings published more than two centuries ago by Mirri and Carletti, and through some very vague traces in situ. The other variants have also partly faded, although to a lesser extent, and where they are better preserved, this is never the case with the whole wall, but only with a part of it. If one compares the engravings with what has been preserved of related decorations elsewhere in the Domus Aurea, then it appears that the drawings on which the engravings were based were generally reliable.

Plate 2.1[16] reproduces an engraving of a painting on one of the long walls of room no.50 that continues the courtyard in front of the nymphaeum no.45 to the south. A strip of roughly 3.00 m. high[17] was reserved for the dado here. It is impossible to tell whether it was originally faced with marble, as the engraving claims. The highly elaborate ornamental facade, which we should assume to have been executed in many colours, composed round a central point and with an extended storey, is characterized by its great openness. The white background visible through the openings suggests air. The main lines of the constructions are accentuated by thin fluted plaster colonnettes with Corinthian capitals, which are partially preserved. This detail is not clearly indicated in the engraving. Different figures, portrayed as if actually present in the room, enliven the whole.

This type of decoration occurs throughout the pavilion. In room no.70[18] which is connected with rooms nos. 46 and 69 which were partially pulled down in order to build the nymphaeum, it is applied to walls that must be older than the nymphaeum, while in rooms nos. 42 (pl.2.2), 50, 53 and 54 it is applied to walls that are contemporary with the nymphaeum. Rooms nos.119[19] and 129 next to the domed hall, no.128, and the passages nos.118 and 131[20] in the same wing are also decorated according to this system. It should be noted here that in rooms nos.

PLATE 2.3:   Rome, Domus Aurea, room no. 33 (after Mirri and Carletti)

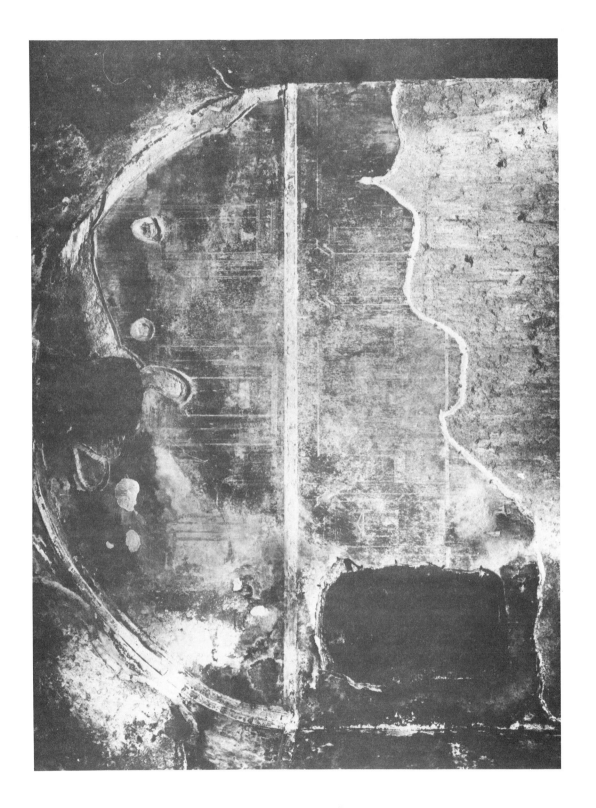

PLATE 2.4:   Rome, Domus Aurea, room no. 23, south wall
(Copyright Gabinetto Fotografico Nazionale, Rome).

119 and 129, painting only begins above a dado 4.80 m. high, so that we are dealing with an upper zone which consequently with lighter architecture. In this stage of the research into the architecture of the building, it is impossible to establish the relationship between the wing containing the domed hall no.128 and the nymphaeum no.45 next to the peristyle as far as the date of building is concerned. If one came to the conclusion that the difference in time is small then the decoration of the rooms in question would not contradict this.

The engraving on plate 2.3[21] refers to one of the long walls of room no. 33, situated to the south of the peristyle. The dado, roughly 4.40 m. high - which is considerably higher than the engraving suggests - was originally faced with marble. Here too, the architectural construction in the painting is hypotactic and there is an upper storey, albeit a much lower one. Below there are three lifelike figures. On the spot, one can see that this ornamental facade was painted in several colours - though yellow predominates - on a dark red background. Originally, the whole must have given a totally different impression from the black and white representation provided by the engraving.

Decorations whose main zones are directly related to that of the room discussed above,only appeared in the peristyle wing, that is in rooms nos. 23 (pl. 2.4),[22] 25[23] and 31.[24] However, on the basis of the relationship between the upper zones it appears that the same studio was also at work to the east of the pentagonal courtyard in room no.116, as we shall see (p.46 and 49).

In room no.42 the two sorts of scaenae frons just described are combined (pl. 2.2). The somewhat heavier polychrome on white is in the central and upper zone, the lighter oligochrome on a red background is on a strip on top of the unfinished dado adjoining the upper zone. Obviously one would be thinking here of a single studio that had several sorts of systems in its portfolio.

The painted ornamental facades in the Domus Aurea were probably created during the somewhat erratic course of building. The inter-relatedness of the paintings provides us with an argument for seriously considering the possibility that the various changes in the building plans were carried out in fairly quick succession, not long after 64 A.D.

In Pompeii no fourth-style ornamental facades survive which can be dated with any certainty to before the earthquake of 62 A.D. What we do have in the alae of the Casa dei Vetti are systems which suppose the existence of the fourth-style ornamental facade and which do date from before 62 A.D.[25] There we are dealing with partly closed-off walls where the architecture visible in the open parts appears to run on behind the closed surfaces. From these and many similar walls it appears that the revival of the second-style ornamental facade in the main zone of the wall, represented in a different manner, underlies the coming into existence of the group of systems which, since Mau,[26] we call 'fourth style'. A clear example of a partly closed ornamental facade is also to be seen in the south peristyle of the Casa dei Dioscuri.[27]

It appears that fourth-style decorative facades were being applied in Pompeii in 79 A.D., the year of the destruction, since uncompleted decorative schemes of this type have been encountered in two places, namely in the Casa di Apolline,[28] and in the house I,3,25.[29]

PLATE 2.5:   Rome, Domus Aurea, room no. 55 (after Mirri and Carletti).

PLATE 2.6:   Rome, Domus Aurea, room no 32 (after Mirri and Carletti).

The latter Pompeian decoration is similar to the group of scaenae frontes on white backgrounds in the Domus Aurea. Otherwise the decorative facades in Pompeii are different from those in the Domus Aurea, and the rooms containing this type of decoration in the main zones of the walls also exhibit a great variety of forms.

Paratactic decorative facades

A very special place is taken up by the decorations in rooms nos. 41 and 55 to the north and south of the large exedra no.44 in front of the nymphaeum no.45. Room no.55 has a dado, roughly 4.25 m. high, but we can no longer tell if it was ever faced with marble. From an engraving published by Mirri and Carletti it appears that the painted decoration on the long walls was based on the picture of a porticus with upper storey separated by pillars into equal intercolumnia, viewed in perspective from the middle of the wall (pl. 2.5).[30] The main lines of the construction were accentuated as in the next room no.50 by slender fluted plaster colonnettes with Corinthian capitals, still partially preserved in situ. From what remains of the painting on the spot one must conclude that the engraving is wrong in certain respects. The draperies above the closed parts were not all looped in two places as the engraving would have us believe, but straightened out in every second intercolumnium. What is more, the architecture in the background is considerably more complicated. Unfortunately the related painting in room no.41, the 'counterpart' to that in room no.55, though in a much better state of preservation, has not yet been cleaned.

These paintings must also have been applied at the time of the construction of the pavilion. There are so many similarities with the heavier polychrome scaenae frontes on a white background that it seems justifiable to ascribe them to the same studio.

What we have here is a system with no parallel within the Domus Aurea. As far as we can tell from publications, it does not occur anywhere else either.

Decorations where the main zone is divided into fields

Now we come to the simpler decorations which are closer to what we usually come across in provincial Roman art.

As for the paintings in room no.32 south of the peristyle to the front, Carletti[31] informs us that they were so well preserved that they looked as if they had been done in his time. We have to make do with vague remains which nevertheless allow us to assert that Mirri's published engraving (pl. 2. 6)[32] reproduces the main features of the original situation pretty well.

The room originally had a marble dado, some 2.00 m. high in the principal space, and some 0.80 m. high in a square extension on the north side. The niche is not painted. The decoration of the principal space consists or consisted of a black frieze decorated with tendrils just above the dado, a main zone divided into black fields framed by broad red strips, and an upper zone with a scaenae frons on a black background. The fields have richly decorated inner frames. The engraving shows centrally situated representations consisting of compositions of Bacchic elements; in the three central fields they take the form of more

or less square 'paintings', while in the two outer ones they are shaped
like vignettes. The vertical red strips are decorated with plant candelabra. On either side of these strips fantastic architectonic constructions
have been drawn on a black background, which seem to stand on consoles in
front of the wall surface and to run on behind the strips, while they
break through the surface of the fields in illogical fashion.

A similar type of middle zone was applied to the rear wall of the
porticus round the peristyle no.20. One can get a good look at the
architecture on both sides of the vertical strips in a reasonably well
preserved, if not completely cleaned, section in the north-east corner.
This again confirms the comparative accuracy of the engraving of the
decoration in room no.32.

The division of the middle zone into panels separated by strips
was in use from the beginning of the second style. What is characteristic of the fourth style is the combination with architectonic
constructions, that is to say with elements borrowed from the scaenae
frons. Such combinations might have come into existence early in the
fourth style, but suppose a revival, in a different form, of the
second-style scaenae frons.

Apart from the porticus, room no.30, to the west of room no.32,
probably also had the same sort of decoration, in this case with yellow
fields, and, as might have been expected in the central location, above
a much higher marble dado of some 4.60 m. Details can no longer be made
out.

With its light construction against a plain background the architecture of the upper zone of room no.32 reminds one strongly of the
decoration of the neighbouring room no.33 (pl. 2.3), of the lunette
and the upper zone of the south wall in room no.23 (pl. 2.4), of the
southern lunettes in rooms nos. 25 and 31 and of the dado in room no.
42 (pl. 2.II), all in the same wing. We are probably dealing with the
same studio that had various systems in its portfolio.

The decoration of rooms nos.30 and 32 and the porticus round the
peristyle no.20 was also applied in connection with the construction
of the building.

It is not difficult to find parallels in Pompeii and elsewhere
for fields divided by strips decorated with plant candelabra. On the
contrary, in the art of the provinces this type of decoration was quite
frequently applied. For the decoration of the fields we have a striking
parallel in. the well-known red and black wall of Verulamium.[33]

However, we know of no parallels for the combination of strips
and architectonic elements which appear to run on behind. Possibly
paratactic open decorative facades, such as those in room no.55 of the
Domus Aurea (pl.2.5), played a role in the combination of the traditional
wall, divided into a series of equal, enclosed fields with architectonic
elements which protrude into the planes.

Remarkably enough, in room no.116, situated in the south-east
corner of the five-sided courtyard, there is no marble dado. The
decoration here is completely built up of painting: a red plinth with
a meandering motif, a black middle zone in which the fields with their

Plate 2.7: Rome, Domus Aurea, room no. 116, north-east corner
(Copyright Nijmegen University)

PLATE 2.8:   Rome, Domus Aurea, room no. 114, north wall
              (Copyright Istituto Centrale per il Catalogo
              e la Documentazione, Rome).

inner frames are separated by architectonic constructions, a still deeper black upper zone with scaenae frons motifs (pl.2.7).[34]

The inner frames of the middle zone consist of thin lines decorated with very delicate flowers. The constructions between the fields have the same rococo character as those in room no.32 and in the porticus round the peristyle no.20 only much narrower and simpler. The constructions in the upper zone are also more sober, demonstrating an especially strong relationship with the aforementioned decorations in room no.32 of the peristyle wing (pl. 2.6).

The decoration is fine enough to make one think of the third style, were it not for the fact that there are clear relationships between the paintings of this room and the unmistakably fourth-style systems referred to above, which can again be related to the rich decoration of room no.33 (pl. 2.3).   On these grounds the relatively simple decorations carried out on black and red backgrounds in rooms nos. 32 and 116 can be ascribed to the same studio which carried out much more sumptuous decorations on red or yellow backgrounds round the peristyle at the time of the construction of the building.

In room no.116 we have a system which, as far as the main design is concerned, appears with many variations in the provinces, though as far as we know, there the decorations of the strips that separate the fields are never purely architectonic. Neither do we meet there the refinement we noticed in the Domus Aurea.

It is striking that the decoration of room no.116 is so different from that in the other rooms round the five-sided courtyard. Most of these have high marble plinths and above, on the small remaining strip, paintings in which red and blue predominate, that is, either smaller scaenae frontes, or combinations of fields and narrow perspectives combined with plaster decoration in the bigger rooms.[35] In the upper zone, above a landscape frieze, the pentagonal courtyard has a rich decoration based on a division into aediculae, accentuated by means of plasterwork, in which the colours red and blue predominate, totally in the style of the famous volta dorata in room no.80, on the axis of this courtyard.[36] This suggests a studio that did not work elsewhere in the Domus Aurea. The 'counterpart' of room no.116, no.64, at the other corner of the courtyard, remained undecorated.

Nowhere in the Domus Aurea are the paintings as well preserved as in room no.114, situated further back to the north-east of the octagonal hall (pl. 2.8).[37]   Here 1.70 m. was reserved for a marble-covered or painted dado. The original plan was not carried out, however. Only in a later phase, probably after the imperial occupation, were the lower walls plastered, though the plaster remained white.

The decoration, polychrome on a white background, consists of two zones on the east and west walls, and of three on the north and south walls that end in lunettes. The main zone on all four walls consists of three white fields, divided by aediculae bearing heavy beams. The aediculae surround vistas on white, the fields all have landscape paintings[38] in their centres, and the outermost fields have inner frames on three sides. It is as if curtains have been drawn in front of three parts of an open construction. It is in particular the side-fields with the inner frames reminding one of embroidered or woven ornamental ribbons that give this impression.

More clearly than in the Domus Aurea one sees the derivation of this sort of wall from the largely open scaenae frons in a number of places in Pompeii, such as the south peristyle of the Casa dei Dioscuri and the alae on the Casa dei Vetti both of which were referred to earlier (p. 42).

The upper zone of the room in question, no.114, is quite like a simple scaenae frons on a white background; the architecture is lighter than the aediculae beneath, but is not dissimilar. The lunettes are filled by a composition of architectonic elements in a style which fits the rest of the decoration.

What is remarkable here and elsewhere in the Domus Aurea is the unity of style within the decoration of one and the same room, at least insofar as the decoration was carried out there at one time. In the Domus Aurea we do not encounter compositions consisting of elements of different designs, such as we see in Pompeii, for instance, in the tablinum of the Casa di Apolline, where only the middle section exhibits a certain cohesion.[39]

Decorations of the type that is represented in room no.114 are met in varied form in the whole series of passages and rooms situated against the slope on the north side of the pavilion, nos.46, 69, 72, 75, 77, 79,[40] 84-86, 92,[41] 141. We are concerned here with poorly lit cryptoporticus which functioned as service passages, and rooms which received little air or light. It is remarkable that in all these rooms the dados were not completed at the same time as the paintings. Where plaster is present it has been applied later, as in room no.114.

Round the octagonal room no.128 triangular spaces form the throughways between the various adjoining rooms. These spaces were faced in marble up to the top of the door openings, but the area above, which was less visible, was painted, like the triangular vaulting[42] with motifs and in a style very close to what one sees in room no.114 and in the series of passages and rooms on the north side, so that it is certain that the same decorators were at work here.

It appears that the group of paintings in question was applied in close relation with the construction of the building, especially because of the fact that the decoration in rooms nos.46 and 69 was partially hacked off to make the construction of nymphaeum no.45 possible.

Highly simplified architecture on a white background is the order in room no.94, situated to the north-west of the octagonal hall in a dark and less attractive part of the pavilion (pl. 2.9).[43] Above the strip, roughly 2.60 m. high, reserved for the dado which was never completed, the decoration has been built up into three zones. Shallow scaenae frontes and other simple architectonic elements are delineated by stripes. Garlands and vignettes of animals enliven the white surfaces.

The room is surrounded on three sides by passages, no.93. In the north passage[44] and the west passage - both with a space roughly 2.60 m. high for a dado that was never filled in - you find the same sort of painting which is nevertheless somewhat closer to the decoration of the

PLATE 2.9:   Rome, Domus Aurea, room no. 94, northern part
(Copyright Fototeca Unione, Rome).

PLATE 2.10:   Rome, Domus Aurea, room no. 71 (Sala degli uccelli),
northern part (Copyright Nijmegen University).

PLATE 2.11: Rome, Domus Aurea, room no. 71 (Sala degli uccelli), part of north wall and west wall (Copyright Fototeca Unione, Rome).

PLATE 2.12:   Rome, Domus Aurea, room no. 46, east wall
(Copyright Nijmegen University).

PLATE 2.13: Rome, Domus Aurea, room no. 72, north wall
(Copyright Nijmegen University).

PLATE 2.14:   Rome, Domus Aurea, room no. 75, east wall
(Copyright Nijmegen University).

more northerly situated passages and rooms dealt with previously.
This is true of both the walls and the vaults.

In the east passage the walls remained unplastered, as in room
no.95, to the south of room no.94.

The two groups of decorations with architecture on a white background, the richer and the simpler, applied in adjoining rooms have in
their execution so many points in common that they can be ascribed to
the same studio, in respect of which we have already established that
it was at work during the construction of the building. This studio was
also at work in the peristyle wing, that is to say in passage no.62.

The simple architecture on a white background shows certain similarities with the sumptuous scaenae frontes on white. Nevertheless,
there are so many differences between the two groups that one ought to
think in terms of two different studios.

Systems consisting of enclosed fields alternating with vistas
which would be ranked among the simpler ones in the Domus Aurea, are
amongst the richest in the provinces. This does not only relate to the
simpler purpose of the buildings, but also to the fact that the scaenae
frons seems to have fallen into disuse by the end of the first century
A.D., as witnessed by the fact that this system does not occur in Ostia,
not even in the more important buildings and larger houses, in the
second century A.D.

A form of decoration like that in room no.94, where the architecture
is simplified to an almost linear pattern is closely related to the type
of painting that begins to be the general rule in the third century both
in the centre of the empire and in the provinces.

Painted dados

In the so-called Sala degli uccelli, no.71, the paintings lower
down the walls were well preserved and easily photographed for a very
long time (pl.2.10-11).[45] That is why they are the most reproduced and
the best known in the Domus Aurea. The charming modern name of this
room derives from the vignettes with birds which enliven the light
construction on a white background. The uppermost part of the wall, however, has received little attention till now. Nevertheless it cannot be
left out of consideration if you want to understand what is going on
here. Above the decoration on white we have just briefly described,
there are traces of architectural painting, probably originally executed
in red and blue, in which the main lines are emphasized by plaster relief-
work, the sort of decoration, as we mentioned earlier (p. 49) that we
meet in more rooms round the pentagonal courtyard. Two different systems
have been applied, one above the other. This can be explained as follows:
very many rooms in the Domus Aurea have, as we have already established,
uncompleted dados and in many places even the bare brick wall is visible
though in some cases it was provided with plaster in a later phase. In
the Sala degli uccelli, no.71, and in the adjoining rooms nos.46, 72 and
75 a relatively simple decoration was applied to this plasterwork (pls.
2.10-14). It was only in the Sala degli uccelli that this led to a
considerable difference between the painting of the 3.10 m. high dado
and that of the main zone. In the three other rooms the paintings of the
two zones are much closer to each other. The oldest painting there

PLATE 2.15:   Rome, Domus Aurea, passage no. 92, arch
(Copyright Nijmegen University).

belongs to the group of comparatively simple decorations in the passage-
ways and the rooms on the north side we dealt with earlier (p.49-50).

That we are dealing with two phases of painting in the four rooms
in question also appears from the fact that, apart from the difference
in style in the Sala degli uccelli, in at least three rooms the strip
intended originally for the dado now looks as if it were a whole wall
with dado and main zone, while in the Sala degli uccelli we even have
an upper zone.

In the Sala degli uccelli the system could only be completely
unfolded on the long walls: above a dado without decoration there is a
middle zone consisting of three fields separated by vistas, and above
this there is an upper zone divided into three by two aediculae, all
on a white background. Slender candelabra, garlands and the vignettes
with birds together with the architectonic constructions greatly con-
tribute to the impression of the whole. The system in itself is a
simplified form of what we saw in room no.114. The execution is far
simpler and is characterized by its flatness. As for the components of
the decoration there are clear similarities to elements in a number of
rooms of the group related to the decoration in room no.114, particularly
in the upper reveals of the windows in the south wall of passage no.
92,[46] under the arch in the same passage (pl. 2.15),[47] under the latei
of a wide throughway in the north wall of room no.77 and in the paintings of the first phase of room no.75, on the east wall in the lower
part of the main zone (pl. 2.14).

In the triangular space no.72 the plinth is ochre yellow and
undecorated, and the main zone consists of fields divided off by
aediculae, all on white, a simplified form of the system that was
applied to the wall above in the first phase (pl. 2.13). A yellow
frame with brown stripes along the upper edge of the painting of the
second phase is identical to the frame between the middle and upper
zones in the Sala degli uccelli, no.71.

In room no.75 the second phase painting consists of a reddish-
brown plinth with above it ochre yellow panels provided with an inner
frame (pl. 2.14).

In room no. 46 the painting of the second phase which has only been
preserved on the east wall, is also executed in brown on an ochre background (pl. 2.12). Two garlands hang within a panel delineated by
stripes, to the right of which we see an aedicula which has been lightly
sketched in. A brown plinth may well be concealed under a pile of earth
yet to be cleared away.

It is remarkable that the first-phase painting below was added to
when the dado was filled in. It is possible that a lower strip was
damaged when the new layer of plaster was applied and that it had to be
partially renewed.

Room no.46 is one of the rooms which was partially demolished in
order to make room for the nymphaeum, as mentioned above. It is only
in the case of this room that we can demonstrate with certainty that
the second phase of the decoration is from the time of the imperial
occupation, to which period the building of the nymphaeum should be
ascribed. Mention has already been made of the colour relationship

PLATE 2.16:   Rome, Domus Aurea, room 42, east wall
(Copyright Nijmegen University).

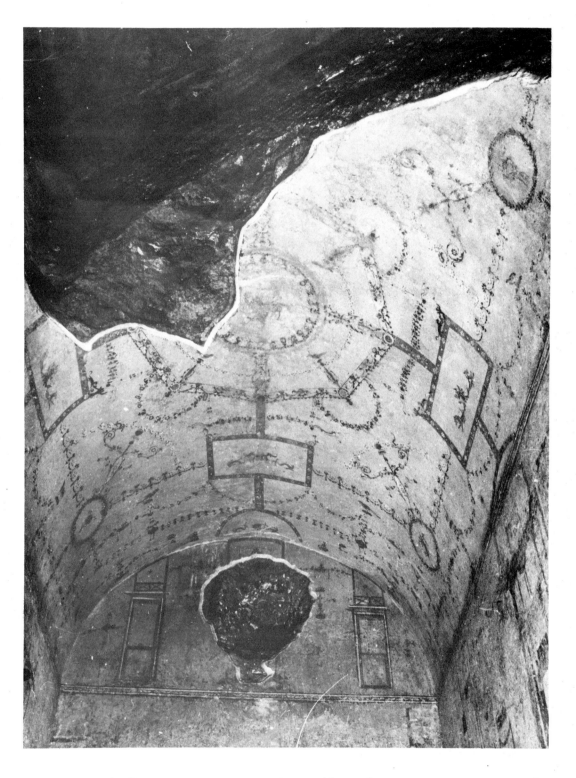

PLATE 2.17:   Rome, Domus Aurea, room 42, vault
(Copyright Fototeca Unione, Rome).

PLATE 2.18:   Rome, Domus Aurea, room 48, north wall
(Copyright Nijmegen University).

PLATE 2.19:   Rome, Domus Aurea, room 48, west wall

(Copyright Nijmegen University).

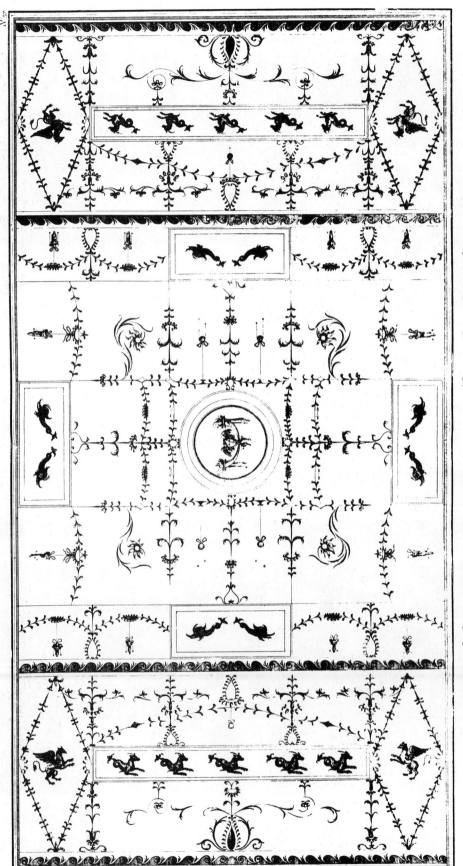

PLATE 2.20: Rome, Domus Aurea, room 48, vault of southern part (after Mirri and Carletti).

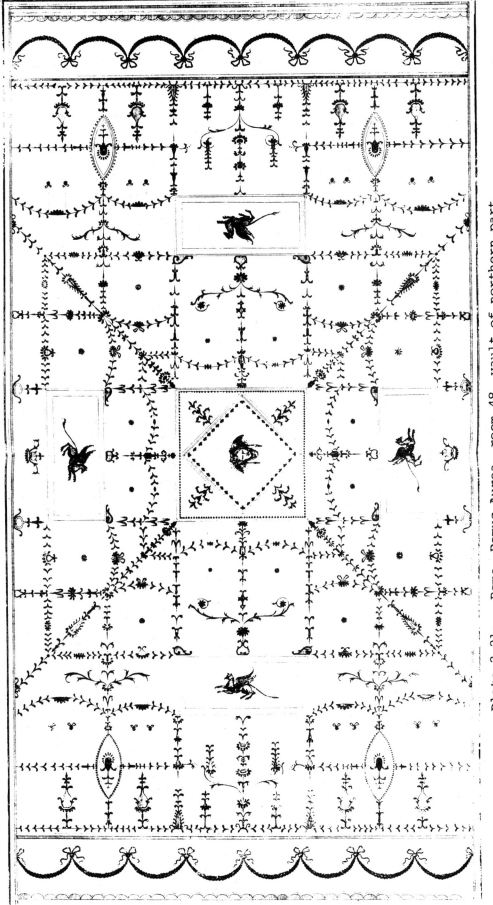

Plate 2.21: Rome, Domus Aurea, room 48, vault of northern part (after Mirri and Carletti).

between the dados in rooms nos.46 and 75. In the four rooms in question there is also the similarity in the careless way in which the uppermost layer of plaster has been applied to the dados. It seems likely that, once the decision was taken to fill the dados in, a beginning was made in this corner of the pavilion. As with so many plans this one too was only partially carried out. The paintings of the second phase in the four rooms in question are most probably contemporary. This would place the famous Sala degli uccelli in the imperial phase of occupation.

The paintings of the phase of non-imperial occupation

Not far from the Sala degli uccelli, no.71, is room no.42, to the north of the nymphaeum. Here an upper storey of one room was built in above roughly two thirds of the space on the north side. Completely new decoration in brown and ochre was applied to the walls and the vaulting of the new room (pls. 2.16-17):[48]   on the walls fields were divided by restrained prospects, on the vaulting floral fringes, tendrils and garlands were arranged in geometric patterns. It is on the vaulting more than on the walls, which incidentally are less well preserved, that we find again the various elements familiar to us from the Sala degli uccelli. The likeness is striking particularly in the case of a little leaf candelabrum flanked by two curling creepers which appears in the upper zone of the Sala degli uccelli and in the upper chamber of room no.42 on the vaulting. Elsewhere there are also similarities with first-phase paintings. The arch (pl. 2.15) and the reveals of the windows in passage no.92, just referred to, and the underside of the latei in room no.77 strongly recall the vault of the ochre chamber in question in terms of its design and motifs.

The very sketchily executed prospects on the walls strongly remind one of the only prospect to be preserved in room no.46 (pl. 2.12).

The construction of room no.42 ties in with that of the neighbour-ing nymphaeum. The very elaborate paintings which were applied at the time of construction were reported earlier as belonging to the period of imperial occupation (p. 42). It is unlikely, however, that this is true of the upper chamber. It is easier to imagine such architectural rearrangement as taking place in the period in which separate phases of occupation came into existence in various parts of the pavilion.

Room no.48 which is also one of the rooms near the nymphaeum, has decorations that must be fully ascribed to the second phase (pls. 2. 18-21). The decoration was partially applied to the back of a wall which relates to the construction of the barrel vault in exedra no.44, and partially to the walls in the room itself which were added later.

While one can see the first-phase decoration round the new paint-ing in room no.42, there is no trace of it in room no.48. Either the old mortar and plaster were removed for the painting or the walls remained bare as in the northern counterpart of this room, no.40.

The alteration of the rectangular space resulted in two lower rooms, a staircase, two upper rooms and a landing. The vaults of the two upper rooms received decoration on white backgrounds as we know from the engravings in the work by Mirri and Carletti, even though there are now only scanty remnants of it (pls. 2.20-21).[49] Judging by these drawings these vaults were decorated in a pattern related to that of the vault of the ochre upper chamber in room no.42 (pl. 2.17). There is also a considerable resemblance in the details. In all three cases the geometrical division is enlivened in the same way by plant candelabra and garlands, and a number of compartments are emphasized by somewhat heavier framing. The slender plant decoration and the animal vignettes again form the link with the paintings below in the Sala degli uccelli.

The walls of the various rooms into which hall no.48 was divided also received decoration on white backgrounds - judging by the faint remnants - with an undecorated or marbled dado, a middle zone divided into fields separated by simple prospects, an upper zone made up of light architectonic constructions joined by areas divided by lines (pls. 2. 18-19). We can ascertain that, as to the main features, there is a relationship with the ochre room in hall no.42 and with the Sala degli uccelli, no.71 but a comparison in terms of details is only possible to a limited extent.

It looks as if the rooms nos.42 and 48 belonged to the same non-imperial core of occupation, possibly together with other adjoining rooms.

In the other cores of the non-imperial occupation very little is left with regard to paintings. What is left indicates decorations consisting of simple architectonic elements on white backgrounds resembling those we saw in the rooms close to the nymphaeum.

The difference between the simplest paintings of the imperial phase occupation and those of the non-imperial phase resides in the fact that the latter group of decorations is of an even simpler design. The systems as such, however, have the same character, various motifs are identical and there is a relationship with regard to the manner of painting. Perhaps one even ought to think of one and the same studio that, after the imperial phase, had to make do with the limited budget of less wealthy clients. This leads to the conclusion that only a short time can have elapsed between the periods of imperial and non-imperial occupation. The paintings even seem to merge with one another. Even if Titus had settled in the Domus Aurea, it is not very likely that he lived in the pavilion that is preserved. The period between the first and the second phases of occupation cannot possibly have been more than ten years. Neither is it very likely that the building was left unoccupied for ten years. In this context one should bear in mind the many unfaced dados. If Titus had lived here, they certainly would have faced them with marble. There seems to be ample justification for the conclusion that it was as early as Vespasian - and this would have fitted in well with his policy - that one started using the pavilion in question for a different purpose.

Conclusions

With respect to the paintings in the Domus Aurea we can draw the following conclusions.

1. The most important fourth-style architectural systems that we know from the Campanian cities are represented in the Domus Aurea in one form or another, with the exception of the carved out vela through which one sees prospects, like the ones

applied in the triclinium of the Casa dell' Efebo in Pompeii[50] and in the upper peristyle of the villa of San Marco at Castellamare di Stabia.[51]

2. The paintings of the first phase can be ascribed to three studios; one studio could apply more than one type of decoration.

3. Within one group of paintings of the first phase there are sometimes a number of variants, ranging from more sumptuous designs to rather simple ones.

4. In the first phase the determining factor as to the choice of a more sumptuous or a simpler system, or of a more sumptuous or a simpler variant, relates to the importance of the room, which is largely determined in this case by its position.

5. Judging from the scanty remains, the paintings of the second phase are rather homogeneous.

6. There are connections between the simpler paintings of the first phase and those of the second phase.

7. There are no reasons for positing a great divergence in the dates of the paintings of the various wings, neither in the first nor in the second phase.

8. When one comes across paintings in Italy or in the provinces that have parallels in the Domus Aurea, one can assume that the dates of the first phase range from 64 A.D., or somewhat later, to 68 or 69 A.D., whilst the beginning of the second phase probably was not long after 69 A.D.

9. The fact that in the Domus Aurea both the scaenae frons and the systems derived from it were applied leads one to conclude that the way of decorating, which we call fourth style, had been applied for a rather long time when, after 64 A.D., work on the wall-paintings began in close connection with the construction which, for that matter, is also apparent from the style of the vaulting of the Domus transitoria[52] the date of which can not be much later than 54 A.D. There is not enough evidence to determine when exactly the fourth style came into existence in Rome. Not even the Domus Aurea can help us here.[53]

ACKNOWLEDGEMENTS

Professor A. La Regina, Soprintendente of the Soprintendenza Archeologica di Roma gave us permission to carry out this research and to publish the results. Dott.ssa I. Dondero, Dott.ssa I. Fabbrini and Dott.ssa I. Jacopi provided valuable information and kindly made the necessary arrangements.

Part of this research has been funded by a grant from the Netherlands Organisation for the Advancement of Pure Research (Z.W.O.).

Drs. J.H.M.P. Mes, Drs. E.M. Moormann, Drs. F.G.J.M. Müller and Drs. L.J.F. Swinkels each gave up several days of their valuable time to assist in the work in the underground chambers.

Drs. S.Th.C. Kolsteren provided the study of the paintings with a firm basis by means of his research into the building history.

Peter Bersch, Rob Gras and Herbert van de Sluis were responsible for a number of photographs.

The text was translated into English by E. Kellerman M.A., and Dr. J.M. Blom.

We would like to thank all those who helped us during the research and all those who have contributed to the article itself. We hope that the benefits of the various forms of cooperation we have enjoyed will become even more apparent when the results of this research are published in book form.

NOTES

1. This paper has the character of a preliminary report. Not all the mural paintings which are mentioned can be reproduced as photographs. Designs on a red or black background are especially hard to distinguish on a black and white photograph and therefore we have left them out. It is to be hoped that drawings will become available in the near future.

2. The excavations were carried out by the Soprintendenza Archeologica di Roma under the leadership of Dott. ssa L. Fabbrini.

3. Second edition of the English text: Cameron 1775.

4. In two publications by Ponce, 1786 and 1805, the engravings have been reproduced in mirror image. Only the first publication will be quoted in this paper.

5. For a complete survey of the older excavations see Weege 1913, 137-140.

6. The following select references may be useful to the reader who wishes to gain a general insight in the topic: Van Essen 1954; Sanguinetti 1957; Borda 1958, 222-225; Zander 1958; Crema 1959, 312-315, bibliography on 315; Bianchi Bandinelli 1960; Boëthius 1960, 94-128; Nash 1961, 333-348. figs. 407-421, bibliography on 339; MacDonald 1965, 25-46, and passim; Zander 1965; Dacos 1968; Lugli 1968, bibliography on 45-47; Nash 1968, 339-348, figs. 407-421, bibliography on 339; Dacos 1969, 5-41; Lugli 1969, bibliography on 43-45; Boëthius and Ward Perkins 1970, 214-216, 248-251, and passim; Grant 1970, 163-185; Lavagne 1970; Lugli 1970, bibliography on 608; Coarelli 1974, 198-203, bibliography on 349; Coarelli 1975, 198-204, bibliography on 349; Mielsch 1975, 40-42, 126-127, and passim; Staccioli 1979, 142-148; Coarelli 1980, 196-202.

7. The numbering on the plan follows the new system which was recently established by Laura Fabbrini. For the sake of clarity we only indicated the numbers of the rooms which are mentioned

in this article.

8. Zander 1958; Zander 1965; Coarelli 1974, 202; Coarelli 1975, 202, fig. on 200.

9. MacDonald 1965, 34-35.

10. Dacos 1969, 3-54.

11. Van Essen 1954.

12. Weege 1913, 229-239.

13. Mirri and Carletti 1776, 30-33, pl.6; Ponce 1786, 7, pl.5; Dacos 1969, 34-36, fig.41.

14. Bianchi Bandinelli 1960.

15. Dacos 1968.

16. Mirri and Carletti 1776, 59-65, pl.27; Ponce 1786, 41, pl.25.

17. The exact height of the dados is often impossible to measure, since the floors have been only partially exposed or have disappeared altogether.

18. Grant 1970, colour pl. on 183.

19. Bastet 1964, 154, fig. 3; Kraus 1967, 209, pl. 134; Dacos 1968, 217, figs. 7-8; Bianchi Bandinelli 1969, 132, colour pls. 143-144; Andreae 1973, 484, figs. 345-348.

20. Picard 1970, 58, colour pl. 47.

21. Mirri and Carletti 1776, 36-42. pls. 7-9; Ponce 1786, 9, 11, 15, pls. 6, 7, 10; Nash 1961, 341, fig. 410; Nash 1968, 341, fig. 410; Lugli 1970, 400, fig. 310.

22. Mirri and Carletti 1776, 88, pl. 41; Ponce 1786, 65, pl.36.

23. Mirri and Carletti 1776, 34-36, pl.39; Ponce 1786, 65, pl.39.

24. Dacos 1969, 39, fig. 56.

25. Peters 1977, 97-98, figs. 3-4, bibliography in note 24.

26. Mau 1882.

27. Richardson 1955, 51-61, pls. 11-13; Schefold 1957, 120-121 (bibliography); Schefold 1962, 105, colour pl.13,1. These and other fourth-style decorations discussed to some extent in this article are being dealt with by W.J.Th. Peters in 'La composizione delle pareti di quarto stile'; forthcoming in *Atti del Convegno Internazionale "La regione sotterrata dal Vesuvio: studi e prospettive", Napoli- Ercolano- Pompei- Torre Annunziata- Castellamare di Stabia, 11-15 novembre 1979.*

28. Schefold 1957, 103 (bibliography).

29. Schefold 1957, 13 (bibliography); Schefold 1962, 126, pls.90-91.

30. Mirri and Carletti 1776, 65-66, pl.45; Ponce 1786, 73, pl.44.

31. Mirri and Carletti 1776, 29.

32. Mirri and Carletti 1776, 29-30, pl.5; Ponce 1786, 5, pl.4; Nash 1961, 341, fig. 409; Dacos 1968, 215, figs. 5-6; Nash 1968, 341, fig. 409; Lugli 1970, 400, fig. 311.

33. Liversidge 1977, 79, fig. 5. 1b.

34. Bastet 1964, 154, fig. 4.

35. Dacos 1968, 217-218, fig. 11.

36. Mirri and Carletti 1776, 75-76, pl.42; Ponce 1786, 67, pl.41; Bianchi Bandinelli 1969, 405, colour fig. 174; Dacos 1969, 20-28, figs. 11-14.

37. Grant 1970, colour pl. on 182; Picard 1970, 58, pl. 46; Coarelli 1974, 203, fig. on 199; Coarelli 1975, 203, fig. on 199.

38. Grant 1970, colour pl. on 165.

39. Schefold 1957, 102 (bibliography). Further discussion of this observation will be found in the forthcoming article mentioned in note 27.

40. Nash 1961, 343, fig. 412; Bastet 1965, 154, fig.5; Lugli 1968, fig.10, fig.12; Nash 1968, 343, fig.412; Lugli 1969, fig.10, fig.12; Lugli 1970, 396, 398, figs. 304-305; Dacos 1969, 33, fig.38.

41. Nash 1961, 345, fig.415; Nash 1968, 345, fig.415; Bianchi Bandinelli 1969, 405, fig.173.

42. Lugli 1968, fig.9; Lugli 1969, fig.9; Lugli 1970, 400, fig.309.

43. This room had not yet been completely excavated when this photograph was made. Nash 1961, 344, fig.413; Lugli 1968, fig.4; Nash 1968, 344, fig.413; Lugli 1969, fig.4.

44. Lugli 1968, fig.11; Lugli 1969, fig.11.

45. This room had not yet been completely excavated when the photograph reproduced on plate 2,XI was made. Nash 1961, 344, fig. 414; Hanfmann 1964, colour pl. VIII, and the text facing it; Bastet 1965, 154, fig.6; Lugli 1968, fig.4 (printed upside down); Nash 1968, 344, fig.414; Lugli 1969, fig.5 (printed upside down).

46. Bianchi Bandinelli 1969, 405, fig.173.

47. Bianchi Bandinelli 1969, 404, colour fig. 139.

48. Dacos 1968, 223, fig.16.

49. Mirri and Carletti 1776, 58, pl.37; 58, pl.55; Ponce 1786, 59, pl.35; 91, pl.54.

50. Maiuri 1936, 18-19, fig.14. See the forthcoming article mentioned in note 27.

51. Elia 1957, 19-21; Grafico A.

52. Bastet 1971; Bastet 1972.

53. Bastet 1964; Bastet and De Vos 1979.

BIBLIOGRAPHY

Abbreviations as given in *Fasti Archeologici*.

Andreae 1973. Andreae, B., *Römische Kunst*, Freiburg-Basel-Wien, 1973.

Bastet 1964. Bastet, F.L., 'Wann fing der Vierte Stil an?', *BABesch*, 39 (1964), 149-155.

Bastet 1971. Bastet, F.L., 'Domus Transitoria', I, *BABesch*, 46 (1971), 144-172.

Bastet 1972. Bastet, F.L., 'Domus Transitoria', II, *BABesch*, 47 (1972), 61-87.

Bastet and De Vos 1979. Bastet, F.L. and De Vos, M., *Il terzo stile pompeiano. Proposta per una classificazione del terzo stile pompeiano*, Archeologische Studiën van het Nederlands Instituut te Rome, 4, 's-Gravenhage, 1979.

Bianchi Bandinelli 1960. Bianchi Bandinelli, R., 'Fabullus', *Enciclopedia dell'arte antica*, III, Roma, 1960, 566-567.

Bianchi Bandinelli 1969. Bianchi Bandinelli, R., *L'arte romana nel centro del potere*, Milano, 1969.

Boethius 1960. Boethius, A., *The Golden House of Nero. Some Aspects of Roman Architecture*, Ann Arbor, 1960.

Boethius and Ward Perkins 1970. Boethius, A. and Ward Perkins, J., *Etruscan and Roman Architecture*, Harmondsworth, 1970.

Borda 1958. Borda, M., *La pittura romana*, Milano, 1958.

Cameron 1772. Cameron, Ch., *The Baths of the Romans, Les Bains des Romains*, London, 1772.

Cameron 1775. Cameron, Ch., *The Baths of the Romans*, 2nd Ed., London, 1775.

Coarelli 1974. Coarelli, F., *Guida archeologica di Roma*, Milano, 1974.

Coarelli 1975. Coarelli, F., *Rom. Ein archäologischer Führer*, Freiburg-
    Basel-Wien, 1975.

Coarelli 1980. Coarelli, F., *Roma*, Guide archeologiche Laterza, 6, Roma,
    1980.

Crema 1959. Crema, L., *L'architettura romana*, Enciclopedia classica,
    Sezione III, Vol. XII, Torino, 1959.

Dacos 1968. Dacos, N., 'Fabullus et l'autre peintre de la Domus Aurea',
    Dialoghi di archeologia, 2 (1968), 210-226.

Dacos,1969. Dacos, N., *La découverte de la Domus Aurea et la formation
    des grotesques à la renaissance*, London-Leiden, 1969.

De Romanis 1822. De Romanis, A., *Le antiche camere esquiline dette
    comunemente delle terme di Tito, disegnate e illustrate*, Roma,
    1822.

Elia 1957. Elia, O., *Pitture di Stabia*, Napoli, 1957.

Grant 1970. Grant, M., *Nero*, Milano, 1970.

Hanfmann 1964. Hanfmann, G., *A Modern Survey of the Art of Imperial
    Rome*, London, 1964.

Kraus 1967. Kraus, Th., *Das römische Weltreich*, Propyläen Kunstge-
    schichte, Band 2, Berlin, 1967.

Lavagne 1970. Lavagne, H., 'La nymphée au Polyphème de la Domus Aurea',
    Mél, 82 (1970), 673-721.

Liversidge 1977. Liversidge, J., 'Recent Developments in Romano-British
    Wall-Painting', in: Munby, J. and Henig, M., *Roman Life and Art in
    Britain. A Celebration in Honour of the Eightieth Birthday of
    Jocelyn Toynbee*, B.A.R., 41 (1977), 75-103.

Lugli 1968. Lugli, G., *Nero's Golden House and the Trajan Baths*, Rome,
    1968.

Lugli 1969. Lugli, G., *La Domus Aurea e le terme di Traiano*, Roma, 1969.

Lugli 1970. Lugli, G., *Itinerario di Roma antica*, Milano, 1970.

MacDonald 1965. MacDonald, W., *The Architecture of the Roman Empire*,
    New Haven-London, 1965.

Maiuri 1936. Maiuri, A., *Le pitture delle Case di 'M.Fabius Amandio',
    del 'Sacerdos Amandus' e di 'P. Cornelius Teges'*, Monumenta della
    pittura antica scoperti in Italia, Sezione Terza, Pompei, Fasc.
    II, Roma, 1936.

Mau 1882. Mau, A., *Geschichte der decorativen Wandmalerei in Pompeji*,
    Berlin, 1882.

Mielsch 1975. Mielsch, H., *Römische Stuckreliefs*, Heidelberg, 1975.

Mirri and Carletti 1776. Mirri, L. and Carletti, G., *Le antiche camere delle Terme di Tito e le loro pitture,* Roma, 1776.

Nash 1961. Nash, E., *Bildlexikon zur Topographie des antiken Roms,* 1. Bd., Tübingen, 1961.

Nash 1968. Nash, E., *A Pictorial Dictionary of Ancient Rome,* 2nd Ed., Vol. 1, New York-Washington, 1968.

Peters 1977. Peters, W.J.Th., 'La composizione delle pareti dipinte nella Casa dei Vetti a Pompei', *Mededelingen van het Nederlands Instituut te Rome,* Nova Series, 4, 39 (1977), 95-128.

Picard 1970. Picard, G., *Roman Painting,* London, 1970.

Ponce 1786. Ponce, M., *Description des Bains de Titus, ou collection des peintures trouvées dans les ruines des thermes de cet empereur,* Paris, 1786.

Ponce 1805. Ponce, M., *Collection de tableaux et arabesques antiques trouvées dans les Thermes de Titus,* Paris, 1805.

Richardson 1955. Richardson, L., *The Casa dei Dioscuri and its Painters.* MAARome, 23 (1955).

Sanguinetti 1957. Sanguinetti, F., 'Lavori recenti nella Domus Aurea', *Palladio,* 7 (1957), 126-127.

Schefold 1957. Schefold, K., *Die Wände Pompejis. Topographisches Verzeichnis der Bildmotive,* Berlin, 1957.

Schefold 1962. Schefold, K., *Vergessenes Pompeji. Unveröffentlichte Bilder römischer Wanddekorationen in geschichtlicher Folge herausgegeben,* Bern-Munchen, 1962.

Staccioli 1979. Staccioli, R.A., *Roma entro le mura,* Roma, 1979.

Van Essen 1954. Van Essen, C.C., 'La topographie de la Domus Aurea Neronis', *Mededelingen van de Koninklijke Nederlandsche Akademie van Wetenschappen, Afdeling Letterkunde,* Nieuwe Reeks, 17, no. 2 (1954), 371-398.

Van Essen 1955. Van Essen, C.C., 'La découverte du Laocoon', *Mededelingen van de Koninklijke Nederlandsche Akademie van Wetenschappen, Afdeling Letterkunde,* Nieuwe Reeks, 18 (1955), 291-305.

Weege 1913. Weege, F., 'Das Goldene Haus des Nero', *JdI,* 28 (1913), 127-244.

Zander 1958. Zander, G., 'La Domus Aurea. Nuovi problemi architettonici', *Bolletino del Centro di studi per la storia dell'architettura,* 12 (1958), 47-64.

Zander 1965. Zander, G., 'Nuovi studi e ricerche sulla Domus Aurea', *Palladio,* 1 (1965), 157-159.

3. THE DIFFUSION OF THE THIRD POMPEIAN STYLE IN GAUL

Alix Barbet
(translated by Anne Gruaz)

(Le texte original de cette conférence a été prononcé en francais au séminaire sur la peinture murale provinciale à Cambridge (septembre 1980) et sera publié intégralement dans une revue francaise.)

Roman wall painting of the period 100 B.C.-A.D. 100 has been divided into four decorative styles; the chronology and detailed classification have often been subject to discussion.[1] The difficulty is that we must find a stylistic and typological vocabulary to describe its main decorative schemes.

The Third Style, which used to be the least clearly defined, has just been studied exhaustively by F.L.Bastet and M. de Vos (Bastet-de Vos 1979). It is generally agreed that it originated in Italy under the reign of Augustus and ended circa A.D. 40-45.

Wall Painting in Gaul

Mural decoration was introduced to Gaul by the Romans, as early as the first century B.C. In *Glanum*, a *graffito* in the House of Sulla, datable to 32 B.C., provides the *terminus ante quem* of 40 B.C. for the wall paintings, which belong to the Second Style (Barbet 1974). We can thus see that in the field of mural decoration the province of Narbonnaise does not lag far behind Italy.

A synoptic study of the Third Style has not yet been made thanks to the lack of published material. The present writer and her team have been engaged in research on a series of mural paintings with common features.[2] Some of them were dated by archaeological evidence, others on the basis of their ornament. We should first note that the Third Style did not spread only to the South of Gaul, but also to other more northerly sites such as Commugny in Switzerland and Champlieu (near Compiègne)(fig. 3.1). In the valley of the Rhône, two important sites have brought to light wall paintings which are typical of the Third Style.

I Vienne (Isère):

A) *The excavations of the "nympheas"*: These revealed mural paintings still *in situ* (subsequently removed) including a frieze of herons on a black background, alternating with clusters of plants. Above is a black open field with a succession of finely decorated candelabra with umbels crowned by flying figures (pl. 3.1). Sealed in the floor of the peristyle were fragments of pottery dating to the Augustan age and a Gaulish coin of a type in use at the latest in the time of Tiberius.[3] Other paintings, notably a panelled dado with

Fig.3.1. Map of chief sites showing the diffusion
of Style III painting in Gaul.

diamond-shaped pattern, tend to confirm that the building is Augustan.

B) *Place St Pierre:* Rescue excavations of a building revealed different phases of occupation. In the upper levels there were mosaics with geometric and figured decorations. The lower levels contained wall paintings *in situ* assigned to the period of Vespasian on pottery evidence from the water-main trench below.[4]

The motifs in the paintings are typical of the repertoire of the Third Style: plants in clusters, delicate and intricate architectural forms, crossed *thyrsi* in the dado, ornamental bands with a pattern of hearts and round spots, very similar to those found in Roquelaure (Gers)(pl. 3.2, fig. 3.2).

II Lyon (Rhône):

Excavations in the *rue des Farges* produced several buildings and a house which had undergone alterations. Fragments of decoration remaining on the walls were dated to 10 B.C.-A.D. 10 on the strength of stratigraphical evidence.[5] In the main zone, which is plain red, there is a woman with flowing drapery reminiscent of the Iphigenia of Magdalensberg.[6] The candelabra are Italian in structure and inspiration. Their bases are decorated with small balls and their bell-shaped umbels are exquisitely painted.

III Perigueux (Dordogne):

Excavations in a cellar produced wall-paintings with significant features. The panelled dado imitates the relief of drafted-margin masonry which is typical of the Second Style. There is no perspective in the main zone, which is surrounded by a leaf festoon. Varying motifs, such as herons, candelabra (one is shaped like the trunk of a palm-tree and recalls a Pompeian model), a band ornamented with hearts and round spots (recalling the similar one found in Vienne), and a medallion with two masks (pls. 3.3., 3.4). Although these paintings cannot be accurately dated,[7] their general pattern follows the trend already noted in Vienne and Lyon and dated to the Augustan period.

IV Roquelaure (Gers):

Only a part of the mural paintings produced by the excavations in "La Sioutat" have been reconstructed and dated between the 2nd century B.C. and the 1st century A.D. on the basis of pottery finds. Stately columns rise from bases decorated with leaves and cubes.[8] They rest on a delicately decorated podium, and we can imagine that there was a parapet or a predella too. An inset panel features a naked Dionysos surrounded by delicate candelabra and a band of ovolo. On other fragments, we find again the ornamented band with the pattern of hearts and small spots typical of the Third Style, but treated here in a slightly different manner.

V Champlieu (in the forest of Compiègne, Oise):

The gallery round the temple revealed fragments of paintings as well as a black and white mosaic *in situ* with the characteristic motif of the eight-lozenge star. From the style of this mosaic and a Gaulish

Plate 3.1: Vienne. Two herons on the south wall of the
'nympheas' peristyle.

Plate 3.2: Vienne. Place St.Pierre. Dado with thirsi.

Plate 3.3: Perigueux. Detail from top of panel.

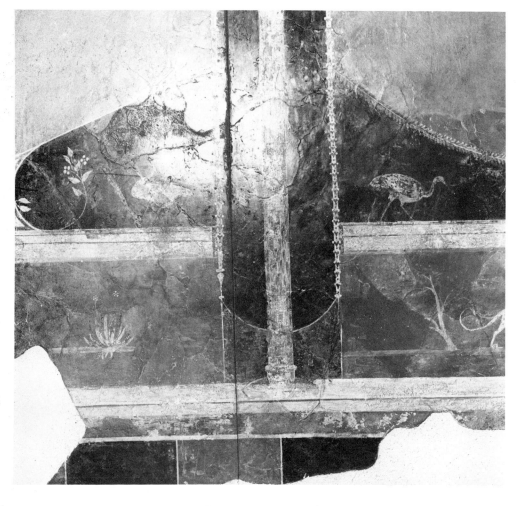

Plate 3.4: Perigueux. Base of panel.

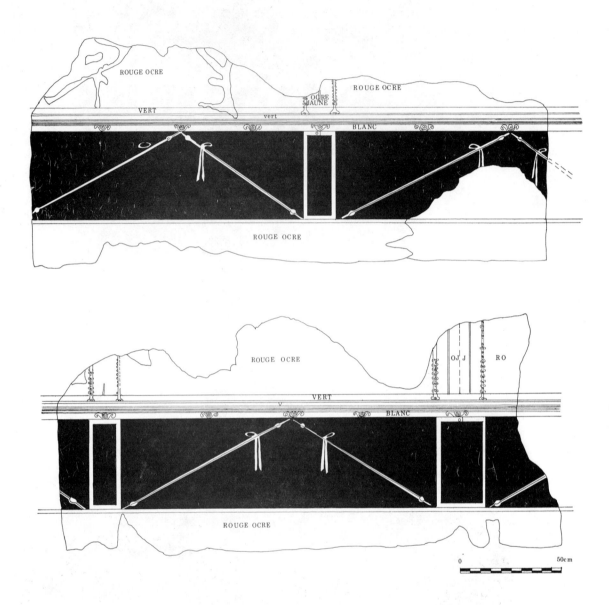

Fig.3.2. Vienne, place St. Pierre, drawing of
the plinth with the oblique thirsi.

Fig.3.3. Champlieu, drawing of the decoration
          of the temple gallery.

coin found near the paintings, we can infer that the building of the temple goes back to the Tiberian period. The fragments show plants in clusters and the leg of a heron. The red panels with black surrounds are framed with black and white lines as at Lyon. The narrow upright panels display candelabra with the motif like the trunk of a palm-tree and various animals on their stems (fig.3.3).

We could quote several other examples of the diffusion of the Third Style in Gaul, but as yet only a few studies on the subject have been published, for the site of Chizé (Deux-Sèvres) for example (Allag 1974).

Conclusion:

In conclusion, we can note that the Third Style, imported from Italy, did exist in Gaul; it spread all over the country contemporaneously with its Italian models (that is during the reign of Augustus, who was a great town builder) and then of Tiberius, and achieved a great success.

REMERCIEMENTS

Pour les peintures de Vienne, nous sommes redevables à M M. Boucher et M. Tourrenc de leur accueil; pour Périgueux, la compréhension de M.M. Gauthier et celle de M.C.Barrière ont accéléré le travail, de même les facilités offertes par M.Soubeyran, conservateur du musée de Périgueux. A Auch, M.Péré nous a ouvert ses archives, de même à Champlieu M.G.-P. Woimant.

NOTES

1. A.Mau (1882); Beyen (1939,1960).

2. A.Barbet, *Le troisième style de Pompéi perspectives nouvelles*, Actes des séminaires 1979, 29-38.

3. A.Barbet, J.Canal, J.Lancha, A.Pelletier, *Découvertes archéologiques récentes à Vienne, Monuments et Mémoires, Fondation E.Piot*, 64, 1980, 17-140.

4. S.Tourrenc, *La mosaïque des "athlètes vainqueurs", La mosaïque gréco-romaine*, IIe colloque international pour l'étude de la mosaïque antique, Vienne 1971-Paris 1975, 135, note 1.

5. A.Desbats, B.Helly, D.Tavernier, *Lyon retrouve ses origines, Archeologia*, No.92, mars 1976, 15, fig. 5. B.Helly, *Etudes préliminaire sur les peintures murales gallo-romaines de Lyon*, Actes des séminaires 1979, 13.

6. Kenner, 1973, fig. 22.

7. C.Bassier, M.Sarradet, *La "fresque Pinel", Vésone cité bimillénaire*, catalogue de l'exposition, Bordeaux, 1979, 68-70.

8. M.Cantet, A.Péré, *Les fouilles du plateau de la Sioutat à Roquelaure (Gers)*, Auch, 1964, 6-16.

SELECTED BIBLIOGRAPHY

Allag, C., 1974. "L'établissement gallo-romain du Vert", *Bulletin de la Société historique et scientifique des Deux-Sèvres,* 2e série,7, 1974, 193-214.

Allroggen-Bedel, A., 1975b. "Zur Datierung der Wandmalerein in der Villa Imperiale in Pompeji", *BABesch.,* 50, 1975, 225-236.

Beyen, H.G., 1939-1960. *Die pompejanische Wanddekoration vom zweitem bis zum vierten Stil,* La Haye, 1939, 1960.

Beyen, H.G., 1956. "A propos of the Villa Suburbana (Villa Imperiale) near the Porta Marina at Pompei", *BABesch.,* 31, 1956, 54 sq.

Barbet, A., 1968. "Peintures de second style "schématique" en Gaule et dans l'Empire romain", *Gallia,* 26, 1968, 145-176.

Barbet, A., 1974. *Recueil Général des Peintures Murales de la Gaule,* Narbonnaise, I, *Glanum,* fasc.1, 27e suppl. à *Gallia,* Paris, 1974.

Barbet, A., 1975. "Le monument d'Ucuetis a Alésia" *La Recherche,* avril 1975, 4p.

Bastet, F.L., De Vos, M., 1979. *Proposte per una classificazione del terzo stile pompeiano,* Rome, 1979.

Blanckenhagen, P.H. von, Alexander, C., 1962. "The Paintings from Boscotrecase", *R.M.,* suppl.6, 1962.

De Vos, M. and A., 1975. "Scavi nuovi sconosciuti (I,11, 14; I, 11, 12): Piture memorande di Pompei. Çon una tipologia provvisoria dello stile a candelabri" *Meded.,* XXXVIII, 47-85.

Elia, O., 1974. "Nota sul III° Stile pompeiano" *Rend. Nap.,* n.s. XLIX, 155-166.

Kenner, H., 1973. "Wandmalereien aus AA/15f", *Magdalensberg-Grabungsbericht,* 13, 1973, 209-281.

Kenner, H., 1980. "Wanmalereien aus T/H", *Magdalensberg-Grabungsbericht,* 14, 1973-1974, 1980, 143-180.

Ling, R.J., 1978. "Pompeii and Herculaneum : recent research and future prospects", *BAR,* Suppl. S.41, 1978, 153-174.

Maiuri, A., 1938. "Le pitture della casa di M.Fabius Amandio del Sacerdos Amandus e di P.Cornelius Teges", *Monumenti della pittura antica scoperti in Italia,* Rome, 1938, III, 1,2.

Mau, A., 1882. *Geschichte der dekorativen Wandmalerei in Pompeji,* Berlin, 1882.

Schefold, K., 1957. *Die Wände Pompejis,* Berlin, 1957.

Schefold, K., 1962. *Vergessenes Pompeiji,* Berne-Munich, 1962.

Spinazzola, V., 1953. *Pompei alla luce degli scavi nuovi di Via dell'
Abbondanza*, Rome, 1953.

Anonyme, 1980. *Peinture murale en Gaule*, Actes des séminaires 1979,
Dijon, 1980.

4. ROMAN WALL PAINTING :
TECHNIQUE OF RESTORATION AND MOUNTING

Claudine Allag
(translated by Roger Ling)

Research workers who work on wall painting are constantly being faced with the problem of conserving and presenting to the public plaster found in fragments. Even when these have been pieced together like a jigsaw puzzle and it is possible to understand the decorative scheme, the treatment of the ensemble and its presentation remain a difficulty. Most of the time the fragments are left in crates in museum stores and gradually crumble away. To put them on display, or at least to store them in good condition, it is necessary to produce a support which will bind them together and make them easy to transport.

The technique of mounting here described has been used for about ten years by Mme Alix Barbet at the Centre d'Etudes des Peintures Murales Romaines (C.N.R.S.). It is of course only the current stage reached in our research into the preservation of Roman painting, and we keep trying to improve the process. Any criticisms, suggestions or information on comparable techniques will be welcomed.

Preliminary treatment of the fragments:

It is first necessary to clean the fragments thoroughly. It is best to do this while they are dry, using a surgical blade which should be scraped over the surface of the painting carefully without scratching it. The backs and the edges are lightly brushed.

The pieces are then stuck together with vinylic adhesive. If the paint forms blisters, the same adhesive diluted in water can be injected under the coating. In any case the painted surface is fixed with a solution of 5% Paraloid B 72 (ethyl methacrylate) in chlorothene (1,1,1 Trichlorethane). If the mortar is particularly fragile, one can dip the whole fragment in the solution.

Fragments are assembled by comparing their decoration and their mortar. Ensembles are formed from fragments which fit together: a graphic reconstruction must take account of all the fragments of importance, even when they do not join, but mounting in modern panels takes place only where fragments actually join.

Mounting:

1) The ensemble which is to be mounted is laid, painted side upwards, on a bed of sand resting on a light board (fig. 4.1); the sand compensates for irregularities in the mortar and enables a perfectly horizontal surface to be achieved. The horizontality can be checked with a spirit level.

2) The painted surface is coated with adhesive: this is the same

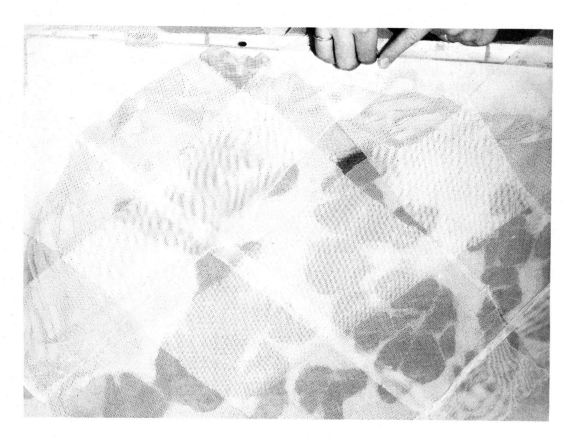

Fig.4.1. Fragments for mounting.

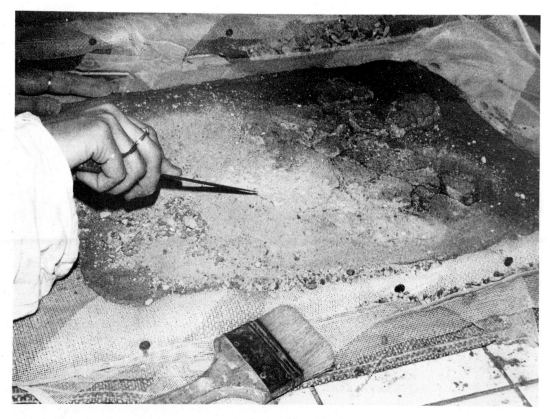

Fig.4.2. Mortar being removed from the back
of the fragments.

Paraloid B 72 which was used to fix the painting, but now applied in a stronger concentration (30%) to serve as a glue. The ensemble is then covered with synthetic gauze, stretched perfectly taut (a single layer at first, then a number of diagonal strips intercrossing to give extra strength). Over this is laid a jute canvas. Both the gauze and the canvas are fixed to the edge of the board by drawing-pins.

3) A second board of the same size as the supporting board is laid over the fragments. It is essential to interpose a thick layer of paper between the canvas and the board to prevent the adhesive from permeating through to the board. The two boards are fixed together by means of clamps if the panel is small and light, or by bolts passed through the wood and fastened with nuts if it is heavier.

4) The ensemble is turned over; the remaining work is carried out on the reverse, and it is necessary to unpin the gauze and the canvas and fix them to the board which is now at the bottom. The board and the sand are removed. Around the fragments, wherever the gauze is visible, a thin layer (3 mm) of synthetic mortar is poured in. The mortar is composed of 3 parts (in volume) of Mowilith D (Polyvinyl acetate), 1 part of Mowilith D O 25, 4 parts of water, 1 part of powdered lime stone, and 12 to 16 parts of sifted river-sand.

5) After this mortar has dried and the fragments are firmly fixed in place, the ancient mortar is removed with a scalpel or rubbed away with a file (fig. 4.2). One of the fragments that has not been incorporated must of course be kept complete as a representative sample. When only the layer of surface-plaster (or a thickness of 2 or 3 mm. if this is indistinct) remains, it is consolidated with a layer of Caparol (fixative L F).

6) A second thin layer of synthetic mortar is spread over the whole surface to make it perfectly even. Before it is hard set, gauze should be applied to serve as a bond with the supporting structure.

7) Applying the supporting structure is the next step: this consists of a sheet of "honey-comb" in cardboard coated with bakelite, placed between two layers of glass fibre impregnated with synthetic resin (Araldyte). It must be subjected to heavy pressure so that the resin binds together all three elements: the gauze covering the mortar, the glass fibre, and the "honey-comb" (fig. 4.3).

8) The panel is once again turned over to be "unveiled". Board and paper are taken off. The canvas and the gauze are damped with solvent (chlorothene) and covered with cellulose padding into which the adhesive will rise after the evaporation of the solvent. This operation must be repeated several times until the adhesive is totally eliminated and the gauze can be removed without pulling it.

9) It is generally preferable to replace the mortar between the fragments with a thin layer of plaster of the same sort (using Mowilith as a binding medium) but with a greater proportion of marble powder (possibly incorporating a little powdered ancient mortar) and rather less sand. We usually leave the fragments slightly above the surface level in order to make them stand out clearly. The edges of the panel are smoothed with a buffing wheel, and the interstices of the "honey-comb" filled with a mortar analogous to that used for the surface-finish.

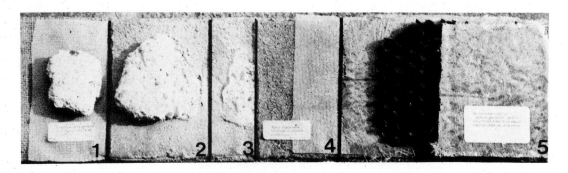

Fig.4.3. Summary of the different phases of mounting the fragments
          as seen from the back.
          1. Fragments held by gauze and canvas.
          2. Thin layers of synthetic mortar keeps them in position.
          3. Removal of ancient mortar.
          4. Second layer of synthetic mortar and gauze.
          5. Honeycomb coated with bakelite between two layers of
             glass fibre and resin.

Fig.4.4. Final reconstruction. Example from Genainville (Val d'Oise).

Special cases:

1) Lifting of plaster from a wall. The method described above is used principally for fragmentary complexes studied in the laboratory. But it can be applied equally well to paintings found in situ. In this case only the first operation is different: the attachment of the gauze is carried out on the spot. To ensure that the glue adheres satisfactorily, the painting must first be dried (artificially if the atmosphere is damp) and cleaned. The painted surface is supported by means of boards. Then blades are slid between the wall and the mortar, or between two layers of mortar if it appears that they will split more easily. The ensemble is removed and taken to the laboratory on the supporting boards, to be submitted to the various operations already described.

2) Painting on a barrel vault or other concave surface. If the surface of the painting is not flat, it is not possible to apply a straight board. In that case, we put a cradling in thin plywood presenting the same curve as the plaster and held in position by battens. This can be used both for lifting plaster in situ, and in the case it is applied to the surface of fragments which have been assembled and covered with canvas in the manner described above.

3) Painting in a semi-dome. We have also been called upon to deal with fragments from the ceiling of a semi-dome, where a simple curved board would not have reflected the double sense of the curvature. Here a different technique was tested: after the application of the gauze and the canvas, the painting was sprayed with polyurethane foam. This substance, which expands in drying, takes the shape of the surface to which it is applied and becomes rigid enough to act as the supporting structure when the plaster is turned over.

It is therefore impossible to lay down general rules; each painted ensemble is a special case for which an appropriate technique must be found.

Graphic representation of the missing parts of the decoration:

When the paintings have been mounted in modern panels, the presence of gaps, both large and small, may affect the legibility of the motifs. There are several possible methods of representing missing elements (trattegio in the tones of the motifs to be completed, painting in close imitation of the original); we prefer to leave the mortar visible and to indicate the main lines of the composition or the contours of the motif in the prevailing tints of the decoration (fig. 4.4). It is above all necessary to be flexible: each type of painting should be given the kind of reconstruction which suits it best.

BIBLIOGRAPHY

Allag, C., Le Bot, A., 1979. "Bourges, la peinture murale gallo-romaine, appendice sur La restitution sur support moderne des peintures gallo-romaines", Archeologia, No.132, 28-36.

Barbet, A., 1974. "Le Centre d'Etude des Peintures Murales Romaines de Soissons," Archeologia, No.71, 40-51.

5. RÖMISCHE WANDMALEREI IN KÖLN

Mathilde Schleiermacher

Das römische Köln,die Colonia Claudia Ara Agrippinensis
liegt unter der mittelalterlichen und neuzeitlichen Bebau=
ung.Zahlreiche Baumaßnahmen veranlassen Archäologen und Aus=
gräber ständig sogenannte Notbergungen vornehmen zu müssen.
Daher sind unter anderem auch zahlreiche Fundstellen römi=
scher Wandmalereifragmente zu verzeichnen: Köln-Müngersdorf,
Neumarkt und neuerdings Gertrudenstraße,Brinkgasse,Pipinstra=
ße/Elogiusplatz und besonders der Bereich um den Kölner Dom.
Hier,unweit der römischen Hauptverkehrsstraße,der heutigen
Hohe Straße,traf man auf die Fundamente mehrerer großer Peri=
stylhäuser,darunter des Hauses mit dem Dionysosmosaik,eines
Mithraeums und eines Atriumhauses.Malereifragmente mit Kande=
laberdekoration und mit Einzeldarstellungen von Tieren kamen
zutage.Aus dem Atriumhaus stammt ein Tierfries,ähnlich dem
Trierer Fries vom Konstantinsplatz (um 275 n.Chr.).[1] Der
Kölner Tierfries ist leider sehr schlecht erhalten.Weitere
Fragmente verschiedener Wände zeigen einen Kopf,Architektur=
details,Ranken und Kandelaber.Einige der aufgefundenen Ma=
lereien waren gepickt zur Vorbereitung für eine neue Über=
malung.Wir haben häufig mit Renovierungen zu rechnen,davon
ist jedoch wenig übrig geblieben.Die großen Flächen der
Malerei wurden meist al fresco angelegt.Diese Technik be=
dingte ein neues Auftragen des Putzuntergrundes,sodaß man
sich nicht selten entschloß,den gesamten Putz mit der alten
Malerei abzuschlagen.

Der günstige Erhaltungszustand von weiteren Malereifrag=
menten und eine umfassende Bergungsmöglichkeit erlaubten es,
Wände eines größeren Raumes von der Südseite des Kölner
Domes zu rekonstruieren.[2] Die Längswände von 7,7o m und die
Querwände von 4,5o m,ca. 2,80 m hoch,waren mit einer Kande=
laberdekoration bemalt.Dieses Wandsystem ist pompejanischen
Wänden vergleichbar.Es gliedert sich in Sockel,aufgehenden
Orthostatenteil und Fries.Die großen einfarbig roten Felder
der Mittelzone dominieren.Sie werden von schwarzen Streifen
mit Kandelabern getrennt,die oben in einen Fries mit ab=
wechselnden Motiven münden.Sphingen,Amphoren und Masken

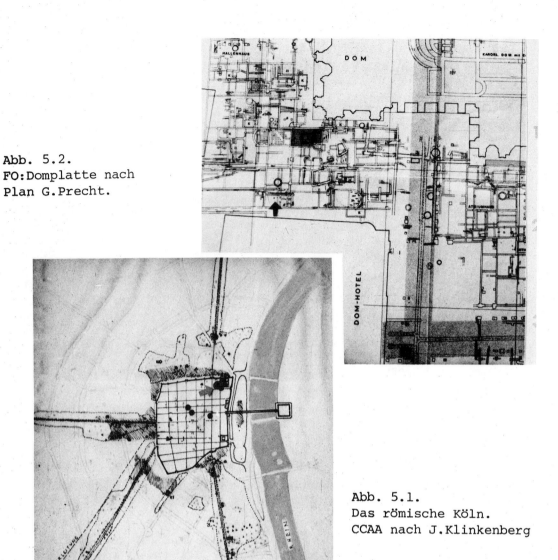

Abb. 5.2.
FO:Domplatte nach
Plan G.Precht.

Abb. 5.1.
Das römische Köln.
CCAA nach J.Klinkenberg

Schwarz–Weiß–Aufnahmen: Sepp Wagner

Abb. 5.3. Kandelaberwand B mit Türöffnung, FO Köln, Domsudseite 1969.

lösen Schwäne,Greifen und Kitharen über den roten Feldern
ab.Zarte Blütengirlanden verbinden die Motive des Frieses.
Säulen mit korinthischen Kapitellen,die die Kandelaber=
streifen begrenzen,und das darüberliegende horizontale Ge=
bälk mit Eierstab wechseln in der Farbe.Unter dem Friesab=
schnitt mit den Schwänen finden sich gelbe,unter dem mit
den Sphingen grüne Säulen und Eierstäbe.Die obere Begrenzung
der Wände bilden grüne und purpurne Streifen.Eine Eierstab=
leiste in Stuck - nur noch die Abdrücke derselben konnten
erkannt werden - vermittelt zur Decke hin.Schachbrettartig
ordnen sich die Sockelfelder im Wechsel von Schwarz und Rot
gegenüber den Mittelfeldern.Unter einem roten Mittelfeld
liegt ein schwarzes Sockelfeld und umgekehrt.Die bebilderten
Sockelfelder werden von kleinen Säulen gerahmt.Den unteren
Abschluß bildet ein Streifen in Altrosa,ca.3o cm hoch mit
weißen,grünen und schwarzen Farbspritzern.Eine fröhliche
Weinlese schmückt den erhaltenen Teil des gegenüber den Kande=
laberstreifen breiteren schwarzen Mittelfeldes.Unbeschwertes
Tun versetzt den Beschauer in die sorglose Welt dionysischen
Gedankengutes: Eroten ernten die reifen Trauben,die ihnen
ein Satyr bezeichnet.Auf der gegenüberliegenden Wand mag eine
verwandte Szene aus dem dionysischen Bereich dargestellt ge=
wesen sein: eine Weinranke,die aus einem Kantharos empor=
rankt ist erhalten,ein einschenkender Satyr und Pan gehörten
hier mit zur Szenerie.In den Kandelaberstreifen der besser
erhaltenen Wand erscheinen Dionysos mit Thyrsosstab und
Panther und gegenüber Pomona mit einem Früchtekorb.Am besten
erhalten ist der Streifen mit Dionysos als Hauptfigur.Aus
einem reich verzierten Kantharos wächst der Schirmkandelaber
empor.Phantasievoll sind die Zwischenregionen mit geflügel=
ten Sirenen unten,mit Panthern und Trauben in der Mitte
ausgestattet.Die Schirme variieren in Rot und Grün,die Ränder
sind verschieden gezackt.Pomona,eine Fruchtbarkeitsgöttin,
hält einen großen Früchtekorb.Das Köpfchen ist ergänzt.Auf
dem Schirmchen darunter sitzen zwei Nymphen.Aus der gegen=
überliegenden Wand ist das Motiv der beiden "Grilloy" er=
halten,das sind Karikaturen oder mißproportionierte Gestalten
wie Pygmäen.Das mittlere Sockelfeld dieser Wand zeigt auf
rotem Grund die Darstellung des Helden Bellerophon,hier

Abb. 5.4
Kandelaber-
wand,
Weinernte.

Abb. 5.5.
Kandelaber-
wand
Dionysos

Abb. 5.6.
Kandelaber-
wand
Sockelfeld
Bellerophon

Abb. 5.7.
Kandelaberwand
Pomona.

Abb. 5.8.
Kandelaberwand
Dionysos

Abb. 5.9.
Kandelaberwand
Detail

Abb. 5.10.
Kandelaber-
wand
Meerwesen

Abb. 5.11.
Kandelaber-
wand
geflügelte
Büste

Abb. 5.12.
Neufund,
Gertruden-
strasse
Gorgo

zum Putto verniedlicht.Er bekämpft die gefährliche drei=
köpfige Chimaira mit Löwen-,Schlangen- und Ziegenkopf.Die
senkrechten Randleisten der Wände werden von langen Schilf=
stengeln geziert.

Eine etwas variierte Dekoration bieten die Seitenwände.
Hier konnte die Wandgliederung mit den Friesmotiven rekon=
struiert werden.Die Kandelaber sind kaum erhalten.Nur das
rote Mittelfeld wird von Säulen gerahmt.Im Fries über den
Blattkapitellen führen Putten Seewesen.Geflügelte Büsten
sitzen über den Seitenfeldern,deren grüne Randstreifen bis
zu den Horizontalstreifen über dem Fries hochgezogen sind.

Die Malerei ist flott und gekonnt hingesetzt.Weiß=
höhung in den lichten Partien,warme dunkle Schattentöne
bewirken Plastizität und Tiefe.Besonders fein kommt die
Differenzierung der Weinranken und Trauben zur Geltung.
Weiße und rote Trauben hängen in der Laube,die fahleren
Blätter des Hintergrundes sind dunkel hintermalt und ent=
falten daher im Mittelgrund räumliche Wirkung,die in die
geheimnisvolle Tiefe des Raumes führt.Brilliant sind Put=
tenflügel - um es an einem Beispiel zu verdeutlichen - in
feinen hellen Umrissen aufgesetzt.Sie bleiben durchsichtig
auf dem dunklen Hintergrund.

Die rekonstruierten großen Kölner Kandelaberwände weisen
vorwiegend Themen des dionysischen Bereichs auf.In den
Mittelfeldern zieht die Weinernte mit Satyrn,Pan und Eroten
den Blick auf sich.Dionysos und die Fruchtbarkeitsgöttin
Pomona stehen sich in den Kandelaberstreifen gegenüber.
Schwäne,Greifen,Sphingen sind dem großen Naturgott zuzu=
ordnen.Die Kithara eher dem Apollon,doch auch Apollon fin=
den wir im Verein mit Dionysos.Masken durften bei den Spie=
len der Dionysien nicht fehlen.Gewiß,wir haben hier Deko=
ration vor uns,Dekoration liebgewordener Motive,die aber
dennoch ihren Bezug zu Leben und Glauben hatten.Der Bestel=
ler hatte sie so ausgewählt.Die griechische Mythologie
vertritt Bellerophon als verniedlichter Putto,der die ge=
fährliche Chimaira bekämpft.Seewesen,von Putten geführt,
symbolisieren Glück und frohes Sein in dem nassen Element.
Sie schließen sich an hellenistische Tradition an,die uns

im Hochzeitszug des Poseidon und der Amphitrite auf der so=
genannten Domitiusara in München (Glyptothek) begegnet.
Eine solche Dekoration drückt die Freude am Dasein aus und
das Geborgensein in einer Glaubenswelt,die dem Leben Sinn
und Inhalt gab und es fanden daneben die traditionellen
Bildungsinhalte aus der griechischen Mythologie ebenso Platz
wie die Überlieferung feststehender Figurentypen oder Deko=
rationsweisen.

Der Grabungsbefund gibt für unsere Kandelaberwand leider
keine so festen Datierungsanhalte wie dies wünschenswert
wäre.Die Wandgliederung mit den reduzierten Architektur=
formen lehnt sich noch an den dritten pompeianischen Stil
an.Gute Vergleichsbeispiele finden sich im Vettierhaus in
Pompeji,[3] besonders in dem großen Gartensaal aus dem frühen
vierten Stil.Auch dort sind die großen roten Mittelflächen
derWand durch schwarze senkrechte Streifen und horizontale
Friese gegliedert,worin sich Kandelaber-und Rankenwerk ent=
wickeln,und wir begegnen in jenen Räumen den verniedlichten
Puttenszenen wie bei der Kölner Malerei.Der Blick in einen
Raum 2.Stils aus der Mysterienvilla zeigt indessen wie stark
man der Tradition der Dreiteilung in Sockel,Orthostatenteil
und Fries bei der provinzialrömischen Kölner Wand verhaftet
blieb.[4] Die Säulenarchitektur ist,wenn auch verflacht,immer
noch einbezogen.Die Malerei einer Gartenlandschaft 3.Stils
aus Pompeji zeigt wiederum Verwandtes:schmale Säulen und
dekorative Pflanzenmalerei auf schwarzem Grund.Die Neigung,
Formen des 3.und frühen 4.Stils zu verwenden,werten wir als
Hinweis auf die Entstehung der Kölner Malerei in trajanischer
Zeit oder etwas später.Damals kam die Tendenz auf,Klassizismen
augusteischer Zeit in der Hofkunst wieder aufzunehmen.In den
Provinzen dürfte mit einer leichten Retardierung der Kunst=
strömungen zu rechnen sein,sodaß wir mit unserem Datierungs=
vorschlag etwa in das 2.Viertel des 2.Jh.n.Chr.gelangen.

Die nächstverwandten Beispiele für unseren Kandelaber=
dekor sind im näheren Umkreis,in Köln selbst,in Bonn und in
Xanten [5] zu finden.Seit Mitte des 1.Jh.n.Chr.sind solche
Erfindungen in den nördlichen Provinzen beliebt.Diese Art
von Dekoration hielt sich bis etwa zur Mitte des 3.Jh.n.Chr.
In Commugny,Genfer See,[6] erhielten sich Fragmente mit

Pflanzen,Architekturdetails und Kandelaberdekoration,die
besonders sorgfältig ausgeführt sind und aufgrund des Mal=
stils und des dreischichtigen Aufbaues in das 2.Viertel des
1.Jh.n.Chr.datiert werden.Wandmalereifragmente aus Kempten-
Cambodunum [7] entstanden nach dem Ausgrabungsbefund um 5o n.
Chr.Sie zeigen Rankenwerk,Zierstreifen,Kandelaber und Wasser=
pflanzen.Unter den Augsburger Wandmalereifragmenten [8] fin=
det sich Kandelaberdekor in schwarzen Streifen,grün gerahmt,
neben einem größeren roten Mittelfeld.Ein Schwan und ge=
flügelte Sphingen bilden die figürlichen Elemente.Die Augs=
burger Fragmente müssen nach der Entstehungszeit der zu=
gehörigen Gebäude und ihren stilistischen Merkmalen im
frühen 2.Jh.n.Chr.geschaffen worden sein.Augsburg und
Kempten sind die am weitesten östlich gelegenen Fundorte
für den so ausgebildeten provinziellen Kandelaberdekor.
Für das Vorkommen in Trier greifen wir das Beispiel aus dem
Palaestrabereich der Trierer Kaiserthermen heraus, einen
schwarzgrundigen Streifen,bemalt in Grün-und Ockertönen,
zwischen roten Feldern,die von schmalen grünen Bordüren
gesäumt werden.Die Sockelfelder dieser Wände tragen die
bekannten Reiherdarstellungen, [9] unter ihnen findet sich,
ähnlich wie bei den Kölner Wänden ein gespritzter Sockel=
streifen in Altrosa mit weißen und schwarzen Sprenkeln.
Die roten Felder tragen außerdem eine gelbe filigranartige
Rahmenzier.Der Ausgrabungsbefund weist in die zweite Hälfte
des 1.Jh.n.Chr.,die Malereien können danach noch aus nero=
nischer Zeit stammen,wie jene aus der sog.Basilika in Trier.
In Nida-Heddernheim [10] kam Kandelaberdekoration aus der
1.Hälfte des 2.Jh.n.Chr.zutage.Aus Vienne in der Gallia
Narbonensis kennen wir einen schmalen Kandelaberstreifen,
nach M.Borda [11] trajanischer Zeitstellung,mit der Bekrönung
eines Schreitenden,der dem Satyrn unserer Weinernte gleicht.
Von dort scheint auch eine Verbindung nach Trier zu führen,
denn es sind in Vienne sehr ähnliche Reihersockel zutage
getreten.Wir haben ferner die flavischen Wandmalereien des
gallorömischen Tempels II in Elst (Niederlande) [12] zu er=
wähnen.Die Sockel weisen eine Felderteilung mit Inkrusta=
tionsmalerei auf,darunter findet sich der gespritzte Schmutz=
streifen.Die Felder der Mittelzone werden durch Kandelaber=

streifen getrennt.Von dem darunterliegenden Tempel I clau=
discher Zeit erhielten sich nur einige Sockelfragmente.Im
näheren Umkreis Kölns treffen wir das Schirmkandelaber=
motiv zwischen der 1.Hälfte des 2.Jh.n.Chr.bis etwa zur
Mitte des 3.Jh.n.Chr.an.Einer Kölner Malerwerkstatt,die un=
sere Wände ausführte,sind noch einige andere Malereifunde
der Umgegend zuzuweisen: Es sind dies Malereifragmente mit
Schwänen aus Köln-Müngersdorf,ein Malereikomplex vom Neu=
markt in Köln mit Kandelaberstreifen,bekrönt von einem Pe=
gasos,Fragmente mit einem Amazonenkampf von der Kölnstraße
in Bonn und Fragmente mit Kentauren aus einem Xantener Hand=
werkerviertel,sowie Fragmente aus einem Nachbarraum dessel=
ben Hauses von der Domplatte,aus dem unsere Wand stammt.[13)]
Auf ihnen finden sich Seewesen,denen unserer Seitenwände sehr
ähnlich,und Victorien.Diese Putzreste waren 1955 zutage ge=
kommen und von O.Doppelfeld rekonstruiert worden.Eine neue
Rekonstruktion legte A.Linfert nach den Ausgrabungen 1969
vor. [14)]

Die laufenden Grabungen dieses Jahres erbrachten erneut
Wandmalereifragmente mit Kandelaberdekoration,mit bunten
Streifen und Mengen von einfarbigen roten Stücken.Poly=
chrome Streifenfragmente kamen in der Brinkgasse zutage und
während des U-Bahnbaues wurden in der Pipinstraße/Elogius=
platz ca.6o Fundkisten von Malereifragmenten geborgen.Wie=
derum Fragmente größerer roter Flächen,bunter Streifen und
Sockelteile,darunter das naturgetreue Abbild einer Ente. Die
bedeutendsten neuen Malereifunde stammen aus einer Villa,
die in der Gertrudenstraße,unweit des Neumarktes ergraben
wird.Sie entstand wahrscheinlich erst Ende des 1.oder An=
fang des 2.Jh.n.Chr.nach dem Bau der römischen Stadtmauer.
Die Fragmente,nicht mehr in situ,waren aus einer Füllschicht
geborgen worden,welche unter einem Estrich des 3.Jh.n.Chr.
lag.Die bisher zusammengesetzten Teile gehören einer Kande=
laberdekoration auf schwarzen Streifen an,die grün gerahmt,
große rote Felder trennte.Die Bekrönung der mindestens vier
Kandelaber,deren Schirmchen einfallsreich variiert sind,
bilden Büsten und Gorgonenhäupter, Motive wie sie in dieser
Form bisher von Kandelaberstreifen noch nicht bekannt waren,
einzeln in Medaillons oder in Friesen indessen schon in

Pompeji anzutreffen sind. [15)] Dionysos, eine Mänade und zwei
Gorgonenhäupter hatte der Besteller dieser Malerei als Haupt=
motive ausgewählt.Die Büsten sitzen auf einem Schirm auf.
Der Büstenausschnitt reicht nur bis zum Halsansatz,von der
Gorgo ist jeweils allein der Kopf wiedergegeben.Dionysos und
die Mänade halten einen Thyrsosstab.Im braunen Haar liegt
ein Epheukranz,weiße Blüten bilden den Ohrschmuck.Sichere
Pinselstriche geben die Zeichnung von Augen,Nase und Mund.
Warme Farbtöne differenzieren die Schattenpartien.Sorgfältig
liegt die Weißhöhung auf Stirne,Nase und Wangen.Charakteri=
stisch erscheinen hier die sicher gesetzten Schrägschraffuren.
Hintergrundflächen und Streifen sind geglättet,in den Gesich=
tern blieben grobere Pinselstriche stehen.Das Haupt der Gorgo
weist dagegen Unterschiede auf.Die Gesichtszüge sind allgemei=
ner,eher puttenhaft gestaltet.Die Lichter sind breit aufgesetzt.
Flotte weiche Pinselführung formt die Rundungen der Wangen.Die
Schlangen,die sich um das Haupt winden und die Flügel im
hochgebundenen Haar wirken in ihrer Stilisierung volkstümlich.
Den Stil können wir mittels der Augen am besten fassen.Mit nur
wenigen Strichen werden sie charakterisiert als groß und weit
aufgerissen.Die Modellierung ist malerisch und weich,besonders
darin liegt der stilistische Unterschied gegenüber der Mänade.
Das Licht fällt von oben links ein.Ein Kopf aus Xanten [16)]
weist Parallelen in der Malweise auf,obgleich die Pinsel=
führung dort kräftiger erscheint.Dieser teilweise expressi=
vere Malstil,- vergleichen wir die beiden Kandelaberwände
mit der Weinernte und die Fragmente mit den Büsten - führt
in hadrianisch-antoninische Zeit.Damals wurden hellenistische
Züge erneut in der Kunst tradiert.Dies prägt sich hier vor
allem in der weicheren barocken Sehweise aus,besonders in
dem Haupt der Gorgo.Die Figuren von der Wand mit der Weinlese
sind dagegen noch stärker dem Klassizismus verhaftet.In den
Köpfen von Dionysos und der Mänade finden sich starke gra=
phische Momente,die wir mit dem Festhalten an der älteren
Maltradition erklären.Viele vergleichbare Details,besonders
augenfällig die Flügel der Schwäne,erlauben es,die neuen
Malereifragmente derselben Werkstatt zuzuweisen wie die
Kandelaberwand mit der Weinernte.
Aufgrund des Unterschiedes der Büsten,des Dionysos und der

Abb. 5.13   Mänade

Vogel   Schwan
Abb. 5.14.   Abb. 5.15.

FO: Köln,Gertrudenstraße 1980
Grabung W.Meier-Arendt und J.Deckers.

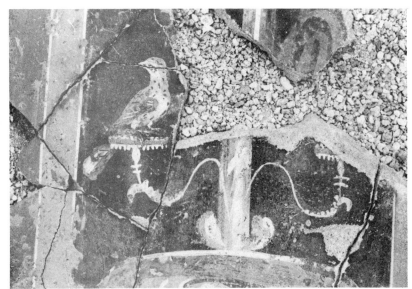

Abb. 5.16.
Vogel

Abb. 5.17.
Schwäne

Abb. 5.18.
Oscilla

Details aus Kandelaberstreifen,FO: Köln,Gertrudenstraße

Mänade einerseits und der Gorgo andererseits stellt sich
die Frage,ob bei Dionysos und der Mänade nicht Portraitzüge
mit festgehalten sind.Es wäre an die Besitzer des Hauses zu
denken.Portraits treffen wir auf Wänden in Pompeji öfter
an.Es wäre dies nichts ungewöhnliches in der römischen Ma=
lerei.In anderen Bereichen der römischen Kunst,bei den Sar=
kophagreliefs und bei den figürlichen Bronzebeschlägen
häufen sich in der zweiten Hälfte des 2.Jh.n.Chr.die Dar=
stellungen aus dem dionysischen Bereich,während zu gleicher
Zeit Portraitclipei die Inschriftclipei auf den Sarkophagen
verdrängen.
Zwei der Kandelaberstreifen konnten fast vollständig zu=
sammengefügt werden.Es bauen sich bei ihnen die Kandelaber=
motive systematisch auf.Zuunterst sitzen auf den Schirmchen
Oscilla ,kleine runde oder ovale bemalte Täfelchen,die zur
Abwehr des Bösen aufgehängt wurden.Ähnliche Gebilde erschei=
nen in dem Fries einer Wand aus dem Nachbarraum der Kande=
laberwand mit den großen roten Feldern.Über den Oscilla
folgen Schwäne.Sie sind nach außen gewandt und scheinen
gerade mit hochgestellten Flügeln anzukommen.Dieses Motiv
ist aus der sogenannten Globuswand in Vienne bekannt.[17]Auf
dem Schirmchen über den Schwänen konnte ein kleiner bunter
Vogel angepaßt werden.Die Kandelabermotive stehen sich je=
weils als Pendants gegenüber.Anhand der erhaltenen Kandela=
berbekrönungen können wir mit mindestens vier Kandelaber=
streifen rechnen.Die Flügel der Schwäne sind in derselben
zarten durchsichtigen Malerei ausgeführt,die wir von den
Flügeln der Putten,Schwäne und Sphingen der großen Kande=
laberwand bereits kennen.Pinselführung und Farbgebung der
Lichter und Schatten lassen sich ebenso vergleichen,sodaß
wir die Arbeit unserer Kölner Malerwerkstatt jetzt noch
besser umreißen können.Große rote Felder,gefaßt von grünen
Streifen und getrennt durch schwarze Kandelaberfelder
kennen wir aus dem Nachbarraum unserer Wand von der Dom=
platte und von der Wand aus Köln-Müngersdorf.Dieser Dekor
in seiner Vielfalt und differenzierten Farbigkeit schließt
sich ikonographisch an die Malereien in Vienne,Augsburg
und an die Trierer Kandelaberdekoration aus den Kaiser=

thermen mit den Reiherdarstellungen in den Sockelfeldern
an und auch im Tempel II in Elst (Niederlande) trifft man,
obgleich früher entstanden,dasselbe Gliederungssystem.Auf
der Xantener Kentaurenwand ist der Rahmen bereichert,indem
der grüne Streifen etwas nach innen gesetzt ist und eine
Punkt-und Strichzier das große rote Feld umgibt.Dieses Ele=
ment fand sich in den verschiedenen gelben Borten schon
auf der Trierer Wand.Auch auf einigen unserer Putzfrag=
mente finden wir eine feine lineare gelbe Umrandung auf
rotem Grund,verbunden mit geometrischer Einteilung,die
möglicherweise vom Sockel stammt.
Vergleichbares findet sich indessen nicht nur im Bereich
unserer Malerwerkstatt.Große Ähnlichkeit weisen z.B.zwei
Rankenstreifen aus Xanten und aus Elst auf,erstaunlich des=
halb,weil sie doch nach der örtlichen Datierung rund 8o -
1oo Jahre auseinander liegen.Zeitgleich und gut vergleich=
bar sind die Kentaurin aus Echzell und der Kentaur aus
Xanten ,[18] fast wie nach einer Schablone gearbeitet wirken
die Schwäne aus Vienne und diejenigen von unseren Neufunden.
Wir erklären dies mit einer allgemeinen Motivkenntnis inner=
halb größerer Werkstätten.Man wußte was gefragt und in Mode
war und man war informiert,denn Handwerker sind wohl auch
gewandert.
Die Wände aus Köln-Müngersdorf,die Bonner Amazonenwand
und die Kentaurenwand aus Xanten entstanden um die Mitte
des 2.Jh.n.Chr.Eine Wand mit Kandelaberstreifen aus dem
Bonner Legionslager,die von einer hockenden Sphinx bekrönt
wird,gehört dagegen in eine spätere Entstehungsphase,wahr=
scheinlich in den Beginn des 3.Jh.n.Chr.aufgrund der zeich=
nerisch-graphischen Wiedergabe,d.h.es liegt damit nach un=
serem augenblicklichen Kenntnisstand eines der jüngsten
Beispiele für die Kandelaberdekoration vor.An diesen Frag=
menten wurden fünf bemalte Putzschichten festgestellt.Die
dritte Renovierung erlaubte eine Rekonstruktion der Deko=
ration mit gelben Mittelfeldern und roten Streifen.Zwei
weitereRenovierungsphasen folgten daher.
Unser Überblick kann nicht den vollständigen Katalog der
Wandmalereien der nördlichen Provinzen erbringen.Es wäre

indessen einseitig, berücksichtigten wir allein Malereien
mit Kandelaberdekor.Es gibt in den nördlichen Provinzen vor=
zügliche Beispiele von Wänden mit Figurenmalerei in den Mit=
telfeldern in direktem Anschluß an die pompejanische Wand=
malerei.Die frühesten und die qualitätvollsten haben sich auf
dem Magdalensberg in Kärnten,in Noricum erhalten.Die Figuren
sind künstlerisch individuell gestaltet.Dionysos,Iphigenie
und Tänzerinnen erscheinen auf leuchtend rotem Grund.H.Kenner
gelangt zu einer Datierung um 15 v.Chr. [19]
Nicht ganz den gleichen Rang erreichen Malereien aus Trier:
der Raub des Goldenen Vließes und ein Stieropfer von der
"Grünen Wand" gehören der 1.Hälfte des 2.Jh.n.Chr.an.Archi=
tekturmalerei ist in der Portikus eines Landhauses vertreten
(stark ergänzt).Aus dem Limeskastell Echzell [20] stammt figür=
liche Wandmalerei des 2.Jh.n.Chr.,späthadrianisch/frühantoni=
nisch aufgrund des Grabungsergebnisses.In eine Wand,deren
Mittelzone durch Säulen architektonisch gegliedert ist,sind
ein größeres Mittelbild und zwei Seitenbilder eingesetzt.Die
kleineren Seitenbilder werden von Pelten gerahmt.Mythologische
Szenen des kretischen Sagenkreises: Theseus und Minotauros,
Daedalos und Ikaros bilden die Pendants der Seitenfelder,
deren Bildgrund verschiedene Marmorsorten imitiert.Fortuna
und Herkules stehen sich im Mittelfeld gegenüber.Sie reichen
sich die Hand,Fortuna hält das Füllhorn.Beide Götter sind
bekränzt und mit ihren Attributen ausgestattet, Fortuna mit
Rad und Füllhorn, Herkules mit Keule,Bogen und Fell des ne=
meischen Löwen.Fortuna ist in den langen violetten Chiton ge=
kleidet,über der Schulter und um die Hüfte liegt ein leichter
gelb-grüner Mantel, sie stützt die Linke auf ein Szepter.
Wir erhalten hier an der Reichsgrenze den Beleg für den star=
ken Zusammenhang mit der italischen Tradition.Der gebildete
Römer liebte Themen der griechischen Mythologie.Daß man die
Wohnräume auch mit den Lieblingsgöttern schmückt,ließ sich
schon an der Kölner Wand zeigen.Die Funde im Auxiliarkastell
Echzell stehen nicht allein am Limes.In den alten Fundberich=
ten findet sich manches Stück Wandmalerei verzeichnet.Erst
die neuere Grabungstechnik ermöglichte es indessen,soviele
Fragmente einer Wand zu bergen,daß eine Wandfläche rekon=
struiert werden konnte. [21]

Abb. 5.19.
Kopf des Tigers

Abb. 5.20.
Kopf des Panthers

Abb. 5.21. Rankenfries

Um die Entwicklung der römischen Wandmalerei des Kölner Raumes abzurunden,stelle ich weitere Fragmente unserer Gra= bungen von der Domfläche/vor.Fundort ist der schon bekannte 1969 Raum unserer roten Kandelaberwand.Die Fragmente gehörten wahrscheinlich einem später eingezogenen Mauerzug an.Die Lückenhaftigkeit des Materials erlaubte erst jetzt die Re= konstruktion dieser Bruchstücke,die,wie wir noch sehen wer= den,spätrömischer Zeit zuzuordnen sind.Wandmalerei spät= römischer Zeit ist in den Provinzen noch seltener erhalten, als die der mittleren Kaiserzeit.Beispielhaft dafür steht die konstantinische Deckenmalerei aus dem Trierer Kaiser= palast des 4.Jh.n.Chr.die die Hofkunst repräsentiert.

Die Rekonstruktion und Konservierung der drei Wandmalerei= fragmente war eine langwierige und schwierige Arbeit,be= sonders wegen des Fehlens größerer Zusammenhänge und der teilweise schlechten Erhaltung.Aus den Bruchstücken,die nicht mehr an der Mauer hafteten,konnte ein Rankenfries mit der Abschrägung einer Türlaibung gewonnen werden,ein Wand= feld mit einem springenden Panther und ein Feld mit einer großen Jagdszene.Der Fries mit grünem Blattwerk auf schwar= zem Grund muß senkrecht gedacht werden,die Blattranken weisen nach oben.Die Abschrägung in Rot gibt einen guten Kontrast zu Grün und Schwarz.Der Fries endete an einer Zim = merecke.Von ihrer Biegung geben einige wenige Stellen noch Zeugnis.Die Höhe konnte nicht ermittelt werden.Die linke Kante des Wandteiles mit dem springenden Panther ist gleichartig abgeschrägt und in Rot gefaßt wie der Fries. Auch hier fehlen obere und untere Begrenzung.Einige der Blätter des Hintergrundes sind denen aus dem Fries sehr ähn= lich.Wahrscheinlich gehörten beide Teile einer Wandfläche an. Das katzenartige des Panthers ist sehr gut getroffen.Er setzt zum Sprung an,streckt die Vorderpfoten weit vor,der Schwanz ist eingeklemmt,der Kopf nicht im Profil, wie dies natürlicher wäre in dieser Sprunghaltung, sondern in Vorderansicht dem Beschauer zugewandt gegeben.Der Hintergrund besteht aus einer Gartenlandschaft mit Blattwerk und Gemäuer.

Von der dramatischen Jagdszene konnten wir das Pferd,den gefallenen Reiter und den aufspringenden Tiger rekonstruie= ren,trotz aller Lückenhaftigkeit des Erhaltenen.In der

rechten oberen Ecke zeigt die Biegung an einem Fragment die
Zimmerecke an,sodaß sich die Szene von rechts nach links ent=
wickelte.Rechts also der mächtige Tiger mit seinem gestreiften
Fell.Er springt auf das scheuende Pferd auf,um sich festzu=
beißen.Das Pferd hat den Kopf zur Abwehr zwischen die Vor=
derhand gesenkt.Den Reiter hat es abgeworfen,doch hat dieser
schon seine Lanze auf das wilde Tier gerichtet.Er stützt
sich mit der Linken hinten ab,um in der unglücklichen Hal=
tung etwas Sicherheit zu gewinnen.Dunkleres Grün gibt die
Bodenlinie an.Höhe und Breite der Wand sind uns nicht be=
kannt,die Maße des Erhaltenen betragen: Jagdszene H 1,64 x
B 2,42 m, Panther H 1,54 x B 1,39, Ranke H 2,oo m x 31 cm.
Wir haben wohl Teile von zwei verschiedenen Wänden vor uns.
Das schließen wir aus den unterschiedlichen Proportionen
der Tiere,des Panthers und der Jagdszene.Der Türfries und
die Pantherwand gehören zusammen,eine andere Seite des
Raumes war mit der Jagdszene ausgemalt.
Der Maler beherrschte sein Metier.Das bezeugen die sicher
gesetzten Linien,die flotten Pinselstriche.Die Malerei ist
indessen flächig und teilweise grob in der Ausführung.Es
dominiert das Zeichnerische.Die Schatten wirken hart,Details
der Gewand-oder Fellwiedergabe monoton.Die Tierdarstellung
gelang besser als die menschliche Figur,die sich allerdings
auch dem Zeitstil fügt in den wenig differenzierten Formen
der Arme und Beine.
Aus dem großen Repertoire von Jagd-und Gladiatorenszenen ste=
hen unserer Malerei zwei Marmorintarsien aus dem Konserva=
torenpalast in Rom [22] und die Mosaiken aus der römischen
Villa von Piazza Armerina,Sizilien [23] am nächsten.Die
Marmorintarsien (Opus sectile) stammen aus der Basilika
des Junius Bassus,der 331 n.Chr.das Konsulamt inne hatte.
Die Haltung der reißenden Tiger dort ist unserer Szene sehr
ähnlich .Der Kopf unseres Tigers ist nur sehr fragmentarisch
erhalten,er war wahrscheinlich in Dreiviertelansicht wieder=
gegeben.Die stadtrömische Arbeit wird um 331 n.Chr.ent=
standen sein.Die Jagdszenen aus Piazza Armerina zeigen
vieles Verwandte. In der Eberjagdszene ist einer der Jäger
in sitzender Haltung mit nach hinten abgestütztem Arm wie=
dergegeben.Aufspringende wilde Tiere kommen mehrmals vor,

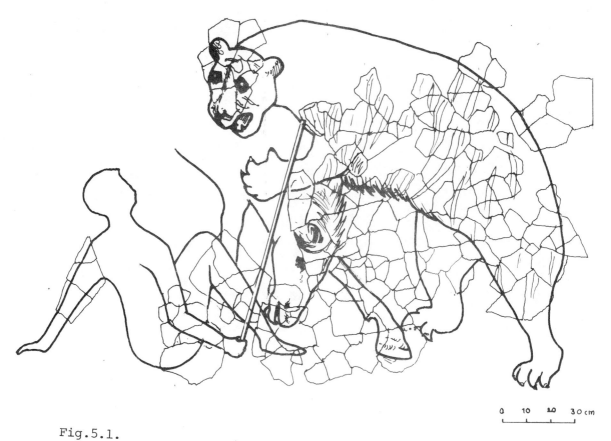

Fig.5.1.

Jagdszene mit scheuendem Pferd und aufspringendem Tiger.
FO: Köln,Dom,Südseite,Grabung G.Precht 1969. M ca.1:15

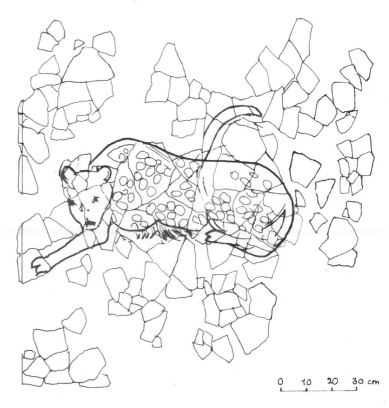

Fig.5.2.

Panther, FO: Köln,Dom,Südseite 1969. M ca.1:15

hervorzuheben sind besonders die Szenen im Hintergrund des Ochsengespannes und des Jägers mit dem roten Schild aus dem großen Korridor.Die Musterung des Gewandes wie bei unserem Jäger begegnet bei Teilnehmern des Wagenrennens in der Pa= laestra.Für diese Mosaiken kann aufgrund stratigraphischer und stilistischer Befunde eine Entstehungszeit in den ersten Jahrzehnten des 4.Jh.n.Chr.angenommen werden. [24] Die Ent= stehung unserer Jagd-und Tierszenen dürfte daher um 3oo oder zu Beginn des 4.Jh.n.Chr.anzusetzen sein.Damit fassen wir eine spätrömische Malereiphase aus bürgerlichem Milieu,die sich sicherlich angeregt von der Hofkunst entfaltete.Die höfische Malerei aus dem konstantinischen Kaiserpalast [25] in Trier bezeugt,welch hohen Rang die Wandmalerei damals ein= nahm.Die kaiserliche Residenzstadt war zum Mittelpunkt auch der Künste geworden,dort orientierten sich wohl auch Kölner Werkstätten.Köln war unter dem gallischen Sonderkaisertum nach den Alamannenstürmen wieder aufgeblüht und erhielt 31o n.Chr.durch den Deutzer Brückenkopf eine Vorrangstellung. Begründet auf der vorangegangenen langen Tradition,konnte sich die Malerei in Köln damals wieder neu entfalten.

Fassen wir noch einmal kurz zusammen:

In Niedergermanien verzeichnen wir seit claudischer Zeit römische Wandmalerei.Aus dem Tempel I in Elst sind jedoch nur wenige Fragmente der unteren Wandpartien erhalten.Aus dem darüberliegenden Tempel II kennen wir die frühesten mit Kandelaberstreifen dekorierten Wände wahrscheinlich frühfla= vischer Zeit aus dieser Provinz.Noch aus neronischer Zeit stammen Malereien mit unseren Dekorationselementen aus dem Palaestrabereich der Trierer Kaiserthermen in der Gallia Belgica.Den Bogen von Süden nach Norden gespannt,erhalten wir die Daten: um 15 v.Chr. - Magdalensberg -,Beginn des 1.Jh.n.Chr.- Vienne,St.Peters-Platz,Malerei mit Reihern im Sockel -,3./4.Jahrzehnt n.Chr.- Commugny -, um 5o n.Chr. Kempten -,Beginn des 2.Jh.n.Chr. - Vienne,Globuswand -,es folgen die zahlreichen Funde unserer Kandelaberdekoration aus hadrianisch-antoninischer Zeit aus Augsburg und aus dem Raume Köln,Bonn und Xanten die sich bis in das 3.Jh.n.Chr. fortsetzen.Die Dekorationsmotive der provinziellen Kande=

labermalerei - Ranken,Schwäne,Masken,Bordüren - finden sich
in Systemen des 3.und des beginnenden 4.Stils in Pompeji
vorgeformt,d.h.,sie waren allgemein in der römischen Malerei
verbreitet.Medaillons mit Gorgo,Silen und Satyr trafen wir
in einem der kleinen Flügel des Atriums im Vettierhause an.
Wasserpflanzen sind in Sockelfeldern verbreitet.Reiher und
Wasserpflanzen,nunmehr stark verblaßt,schmücken den Sockel
der Portikus des Peristylhofes im Hause Menanders,Pompeji.
Dies möchte ein Hinweis darauf sein,die provinzielle Malerei
mit Kandelaberdekoration nicht allzu separat,nur als Anhäng=
sel zu betrachten,sie ist vielmehr eingebunden in die Gesamt=
tradition der römischen Malerei zu sehen.Dasselbe gilt natur=
gemäß für die Malereifunde mit figürlichen Szenen aus Trier
und Echzell und wie wir sahen,für die Themen der spätrömi=
schen Malereiphase um 300 n.Chr.,die wir mit der Rekonstruk=
tion der Kölner Jagdszene aus einem Bürgerhause erfassen.
Die Trierer Malereien aus dem konstantinischen Kaiserpalast
geben Zeugnis von der hohen Qualität der Hofkunst jener
Epoche.Auch wenn wir uns damit abfinden müssen,daß der grö=
ßere Teil römischer Wandmalerei nicht erhalten ist,so bleibt
eine beachtliche Anzahl von Fragmenten,die uns eine Vorstel=
lung von der Vielfalt und dem Reichtum der römischen Wand=
malerei in den nördlichen Provinzen vermitteln.

Technologie und Konservierung

Die römischen Wandmalereien waren in kombinierter Fresco-
Seccotechnik ausgeführt worden.Das bestätigen die naturwis=
senschaftlichen Untersuchungen,[26] auch für die Kölner Kande=
laberwände mit den großen roten Feldern.E.Denninger,Institut
für Technologie der Malerei,Stuttgart,gelang es,an Proben der
roten Malschicht eine Glutaminsäurereaktion nachzuweisen.
Diese Aminosäure kommt in tierischen Leimen vor.Die Konzen=
tration der Leimlösung soll nach Versuchen Denningers 2%
nicht überschreiten,damit zu hohe Spannung der Malschicht
vermieden wird.Leim geht mit dem Calciumhydroxyd des Kalk=
mörtels eine sehr feste Bindung ein.Als Bindemittel wäre
auch Kalkkasein zu erwarten.Kalkkasein wurde anhand einer
chromatographischen Bindemittelanalyse z.B.inFarbschichten
der Echzeller Malereien festgestellt.[27] Bei den römischen

Wänden von Hölstein,Münsingen und Trier vermutet man Leim=
zusatz zu den Farben,bei denjenigen von Augsburg und Kempten
dagegen Frescotechnik.Die Wände in den gallorömischen Tem=
peln von Elst können,wie J.E.A.Bogaers vorschlägt,in Kalk=
malerei ausgeführt sein,die großen Flächen al fresco,die
kleinteiligen Ornamente in Kalksecco.In Farb-und Stuckschich=
ten finden sich geringe organische Spuren,besonders in Schwarz
und Rot,aber auch in anderen Farblagen.[28] Schon früher mach=
te man diesbezügliche Beobachtungen an den Wandmalereifunden
von Köln-Müngersdorf und die laufenden chemischen Untersu=
chungen des Istituto Centrale del Restauro in Rom erbringen
für Fragmente aus Rom ein ähnliches Ergebnis.[29] Organische
Bindemittel sind chemisch nur sehr schwer feststellbar an
diesen Objekten und geringe organische Spuren an Bruchstücken,
die im Boden lagerten,lassen noch nicht sicher auf die tech=
nische Ausführung der Malerei schließen,denn Verunreinigungen
oder Infiltrationen aus der umgebenden Erdschicht können
die Untersuchungsergebnisse beeinträchtigen.[30] Das Fehlen
von organischen Spuren wäre auch häufig damit zu erklären,
daß sich solche Reste verflüchtigt haben.Zu fragen wäre
ferner,inwieweit sich durch analytische Verfahren,bei so
geringen Spuren der Unterschied zwischen tierischem Leim
und Kalkkasein feststellen läßt.Sinnvoll ist es,zur Klärung
der anstehenden Fragen naturwissenschaftliche Untersuchungen
mit praktisch-experimentellen Forschungsarbeiten zu koordi=
nieren.
An den Kölner Fragmenten wurden Untersuchungen mit dem Raster=
elektronenmikroskop in der Kombination mit energiedispersiver
Mikroanalyse vorgenommen.[31] Für Untersuchungen am Raster=
elektronenmikroskop werden keine Zwischenpräparierungen not=
wendig,das Originalmaterial selbst wird abgebildet.Bis zu
1o ooo-facher Vergrößerung wird eine Schärfentiefe erreicht,
die bei anderen Abbildungsverfahren nicht möglich ist.
Das Röntgenbeugungsdiagramm nach Debye-Scherrer erbrachte
die Identifizierung der Farbpigmente.Alle, außer Schwarz,-
also Rot,Gelb,Grün,Blau,Weiß, waren kristallin.Schwarz lag
als Kohlenstoff vor: Ruß oder ähnliches;Rot - roter Ocker;
Grün - grüne Erde,Seladonit;Gelb - Ocker,Eisenhydroxyd;Blau -
Ägyptischblau,Kupfer-Calcium-Silikat;Weiß - Calciumcarbonat.

Zinnober war nicht verwendet worden bei den untersuchten
Fragmenten,das Blau nur äußerst sparsam.Beide Pigmente
waren sehr teuer.Die rote Malschicht der großen Panneaux
ist durchsetzt von Calcitkristallen,dem Pigment wurde Mar=
mormehl beigemischt.Die zugesetzten Marmorteilchen variieren
in der Größe zwischen 1,5 und 0,01 mm.Durch diesen Zusatz
streckte man die Malfarbe,die Malschicht wurde außerdem
fester und widerstandsfähiger.Gewiß tragen die Marmorpar=
tikelchen auch zu dem Glanz bei,der an den pompejanischen
Wandmalereiflächen bewundert wird,und der auch an den roten
Feldern der Kölner Malerei vorhanden ist.Der Glanz ist jedoch
nicht durch Schleifen der Flächen mit feinem Marmorstaub
zu erklären,wie zuletzt W.Klinkert [32] vertrat.L.und
P.Mora [33] fanden durch experimentelle Versuche heraus,daß
das feste Andrücken,bzw.Glätten der noch feuchten Malschicht
mit Spachtel oder Kelle unter gewissen Voraussetzungen den
Glanz ergibt.Dabei spielen die Farbpigmente eine wichtige
Rolle: Erdfarben wie Ocker,gebrannter Ocker,Grüne Erde,
Weiß, basieren auf Tonen.Schon in vorrömischer Zeit hatte
man bei der Keramikherstellung die Wirkung der Glanztone
entdeckt.Durch das feste Andrücken der Oberfläche und die
Wasserverdunstung gelangen feinste Partikelchen nach außen,
verdichten die Schicht und bewirken den Glanz.In der parallel
geschichteten Anordnung der Tonminerale gibt sich eine
Schichtdoppelbrechung zu erkennen.Der schwarze Fries der
Kölner Malereien glänzte nicht.Die schwarze Malschicht ist
extrem dünn,nur 5-10 μm, Rot dagegen 200-500 μm. Man hätte
das Gleitmittel,z.B. Kaolin,das auch der schwarzen Rußfarbe
Glanz verlieh,vorher zugeben müssen,weil im Schwarz die
tonigen Bestandteile fehlen.Wenn das Spektrum bei der Rönt=
genmikroanalyse Calcium und Silicium auch im Schwarz an=
zeigte,so kann bei der dünnen Farbschicht die Feinputz=
schicht darunter miterfaßt worden sein.Der naturwissen=
schaftliche Nachweis für die Richtigkeit der von Mora ge=
fundenen Erklärung für den Glanz der Malschicht römischer
Wandmalereien liegt in dem feststellbaren Anteil von Si=
licium und Aluminium,der in Tonen (wasserhaltiges Aluminium=
silikat) und daher auch in Erdfarben enthalten ist.Anteile
von Silicium und Aluminium konnten in Malereien von Pompeji,

von Kasanlak (Bulgarien),von Münsing und Hölstein (Schweiz)
und von Köln nachgewiesen werden.In den Kölner Malereien
in den roten und grünen Malschichten.Im Ocker fand sich
Kaolinit,Calcit,Quarz und Tonminerale.
Bei der Herstellung des Putzes hielt man sich in Köln nicht
an die Weisungen Vitruvs,sechs Putzschichten aufzutragen.
Höchstens drei,oft nur zwei Putzschichten sind feststell=
bar.Sehr grobe Zuschläge liegen manchmal bis dicht unter
der Malschicht.Marmormehl war in Köln gelegentlich für die
oberste Feinputzschicht verwandt worden,sonst Rheinsand
und Kalk.Eine Wand aus dem Nachbarraum der Malerei mit den
roten Panneaux wies in der Mitte der Mörtelschicht einen
rötlichen Streifen aus Ziegelmehl auf.Durch den Ziegelzu=
schlag wird der Mörtel noch haltbarer,weil das Wasser lang
samer verdunstet,der Mörtel daher besser durchcarbonati=
siert.Erwähnenswert ist die Struktur der Rückseite.Der Putz
war auf eine Lehmschicht aufgetragen worden,die zur besse=
ren Haftung des Mörtels mit Riefen versehen worden war.
Die in unterschiedlicher Größe und Höhe erhaltenen Bruch=
stücke wurden nach Grabungskisten auf Tischen ausgebreitet
und zusammengesetzt,was sich als äußerst zeitaufwendig und
langwierig erwies.
Folgende Probleme stellten sich für die Konservierung:
Die Fragmente auf einer Länge von acht bzw.vier m in eine
Ebene zu bekommen, die in unterschiedlichen Höhen erhalte=
ne Putzstärke gleichmäßig auf acht mm abzuarbeiten, aus=
reichende Festigkeit zu erzielen, das Aussehen der Origi=
nalstücke zu erhalten, die Reversibilität der Restaurie=
rungsmaßnahmen zu beachten, transportable Tableaux zu er=
stellen ohne die Originalstücke gewaltsam trennen zu müs=
sen.Der Putz war so brüchig,daß man sich vor Beginn der
Konservierungsarbeiten zur Festigung mit dem Härtefluat
Laosin B [34)]entschloß.Jetzt erst war es möglich,die Sin=
terkrusten,die die Malerei an vielen Stellen bedeckten
und die sich fest mit der Malschicht verbunden hatten,
mittels eines Korundscheibchens abzuschleifen.Die ca.acht
m lange Wand teilten wir in sechs Felder.Für die Fugentren=
nung wählten wir die Stellen aus,die sich durch die vorhan=
denen Brüche dafür anboten.Anhand einer Rekonstruktions=

zeichnung,die wir vorher von den zusammengesetzten Bruch=
stücken angefertigt hatten,verlegten wir die Fragmente in
dafür bereitgestellte Kästen mit einer Füllung von Vermi=
kulith-Kaminisolierung.[35)]Dieses Material hat den Vorteil,
viel leichter als Sand zu sein,und daher das spätere Drehen
der Kästen weniger aufwendig zu machen.Als Richtlinie bot
sich ein Streifen des Randdekors an.Wir überspannten alle
sechs Kästen mit einer Perlonschnur und richteten die Frag=
mente unter Berücksichtigung der Anpassungen danach aus.
Wo es erforderlich schien,klebten wir die mit Mowilith 35/73
(Farbwerke Hoechst) in Nitroverdünnung gehärteten Bruch=
stellen mit Ago-Goldsiegel (Degussa/Hanau).Mit der Wasser=
waage brachten wir die Fragmente in eine Ebene.Die Fixierung
und Festigung der Malschicht erfolgte mit Paraloid B 72
(Rohm & Haas,Philadelphia) gelöst in Nitroverdünnung.Para=
loid ist eine Polyacrylverbindung in Lösung,die nur einen
matten Film auf der Oberfläche bildet,der das Aussehen der
Malerei nicht störend verändert,sondern die Farben eher noch
etwas intensiviert und der löslich bleibt nach dem Altern.
Die dreifache Überklebung mit zwei feinen und einem groben
Treviragewebe nahmen wir mit der gleichen Lösung in stär=
kerer Konsistenz vor.Nach dem Trocknen der Stoffüberklebung
ist die Malschicht so bruchsicher,daß die Kästen mit Deckeln
verschraubt und auf die Bildseite gedreht werden können.
Vorsichtshalber deckt man die Malerei noch mit einer Poly=
äthylenfolie ab,damit nicht Klebstoffreste nach außen drin=
gen.Böden und Seitenwände der Kästen wurden danach entfernt,
das Füllmaterial herausgenommen und der Putz abgeschliffen.
Das läßt sich schonend am besten mit dem Ultraschall-Meißel
durchführen (KLM-Ultraschall-GmbH.,Weinheim/Bergstr.).Für
ein nochmaliges Härten des antiken Mörtels von der Rück=
seite verwendeten wir Primal AC 33,eine Acrylemulsion
(Rohm & Haas,Philadelphia).Die aufgetragene 4 mm starke
Ausgleichsmörtelschicht bestand aus drei Teilen Quarzsand,
einem Teil Sumpfkalk und 10% einer Mischung aus Mowilith
D 5o und D o25 zu gleichen Teilen.Über die getrocknete
Mörtelschicht klebten wir ein stärkeres Armierungsgewebe.
Dieses kann bei Bedarf mit Nitroverdünnung gelöst werden,
sodaß die Restaurierung reversibel bleibt.Leichtbauplatten,

hergestellt aus Wabenpapier (Stempel AG,Dietzenbach),Glas=
faser und Araldit (Ciba-Geigy AG,Basel) wurden abschlie=
ßend mit den Rückseiten der Malerei verbunden.Nach dem Aus=
härten wurde die montierte Malerei gedreht und sodann in
profilierte Stahlrahmen eingehängt.Den nächsten Arbeitsgang
bildete das sorgfältige Freilegen der Bildseite.Watte mit
Nitroverdünnung getränkt,wurde auf die zuvor gut angelöste
Stoffüberklebung der Malfläche verteilt und über Nacht mit
Polyäthylenfolie abgedeckt.Tags darauf konnten wir die
Stoffe mühelos und ohne Farbverluste abnehmen.[36] Zum Aus=
füllen der Fehlstellen verwendeten wir Mowilithmörtel,dem
wir in der unteren Schicht grobe Zuschläge beimengten.Be=
sondere Sorgfalt erforderte es,die feinen Fugen zwischen
den Originalstücken auszuspachteln und die Mörtelmasse mit
deren Kanten zu verbinden; unschöne Übergänge hätten sonst
den Gesamteindruck beeinträchtigt.Die Mörtelergänzung soll=
te 2 mm niedriger als die Bildoberfläche liegen.Dadurch er=
reichten wir,daß die Farbrekonstruktionen die volle Leucht=
kraft der antiken Originalfarben erhalten können ,gleich=
zeitig aber die erhaltenen Fragmente genügend gegen die
ergänzten Teile abgesetzt bleiben.Das Ausmalen der Ergän=
zungen führten wir mit Farbsortimenten der Amphibolin-Werke
(Robert Murjahn,Ober-Ramstadt) aus, die hohe Lichtechtheit
garantieren.Die Originalfragmente wurden in ihrem Erhaltungs=
zustand belassen.Auf diese Weise kann dem Beschauer die
ehemalige Farbwirkung sehr gut vor Augen geführt werden.
Die Jagdszene dagegen soll wegen der großen Lücken und
Fehlstellen als Strichzeichnung auf einem den Fragmenten
angepaßten Farbton ergänzt werden,nur die äußeren Konturen
sollen in diesem Falle die fehlenden Partien der Szene
wiedergeben.

Anmerkungen

1) Vgl.R.Schindler,Führer durch das Landesmuseum Trier, Trier 198o,98 Abb.314.

2) Vgl.A.Linfert,Kölner Jb.13,1972/73,65-76.Grabung 1969 RGM.

3) Th.Kraus,Lebendiges Pompeji,Köln 1977,Taf.11o,- großer Gartensaal im Haus der Vettier.

4) Ders.,Lebendiges Pompeji,Köln 1977,Taf.293,Villa dei Misteri,Raum 15 und im folgenden Taf.297,Gartenland= schaft aus der casa del frutteto.

5) Köln: J.Klinkenberg und K.Würth in F.Fremersdorf,Der rö= mische Gutshof Köln-Müngersdorf,Berlin und Leipzig 1933, 55-64;Neumarkt: F.Fremersdorf,Germania 14,193o,1o6 f.; Domplatte: O.Doppelfeld,Kölner Jb.6,1961,159 und ders. Wallraf Richartz Jb.18,1956,17 ff.;Bonn: H.G.Horn,Das Rheinische Landesmuseum Bonn,2,1973,19-22,Kandelaber mit Sphinx;Ders.,Das Rheinische Landesmuseum Bonn,6,1971, 85-88;Xanten: E.Künzl,Das Rheinische Landesmuseum Bonn, 3,1969,38 f.; H.G.Horn,Das Rheinische Landesmuseum Bonn, 5,1971,68-72.

6) W.Drack,Die römische Wandmalerei der Schweiz,Basel 195o, Taf.1-6, S.14,26,68 ff.

7) K.Parlasca,in W.Krämer,Cambodunumforschungen 1953-I,Kall= münz 1957,93-1o2,Taf.3o-33.

8) Ders.,Römische Wandmalerei in Augsburg,Kallmünz 1956.

9) W.Reusch,Trierer Zeitschrift 29,1966,187-216,Taf.A.

1o) I.Huld-Zetsche,Nassauische Annalen 9o,1979,5-38,bes.S.21, Abb.5 und 6.

11) M.Borda,La Pittura romana,Mailand 1958,S.94 Abb.S.93, Vienne,Globuswand;A.Barbet,in Peinture murale en Gaule, Actes des Séminaires 1979,Dijon 198o,36,römische Wand= malereifunde,Place St.Pierre,Vienne.

12) E.A.Th.Bogaers,De gallo-romeinse Tempels te Elst in de Over-Betuve,S'Gravenhage 1955,1o4-124.

13) O.Doppelfeld,wie in Anm.5.

14) A.Linfert,Römische Wandmalerei,Köln 1975,Abb.36.

15) Z.B.Gorgonenhaupt,Silen-und Satyrköpfe in Medaillons in einem Flügel des Atriums im Vettierhaus, Portraits und Büsten in einem Fries über Muschelbaldachinen im Lararium der casa dell'Ara massima (Ins.15,Nr.16.)

16) H.G.Horn,Das Rheinische Landesmuseum Bonn,5,1971,71.

17) M.Borda,wie Anm.11.

18) H.G.Horn,wie Anm.16;D.Baatz,Germania 46,1968,Taf.9.

19) H.Kenner,in Die Ausgrabungen auf dem Magdalensberg,
    1969-1972,Klagenfurt 1973,2o9-281.

2o) D.Baatz,Germania 46,1968,4o-52.

21) Ders.,Germania 46,1968,5o.

22) W.Zschietzschmann,Römische Kunst,Frankfurt 1968,Taf.173.

23) G.V.Gentili,La villa romana di Piazza Armerina,Milano,
    Roma 1959.

24) K.M.D.Dunbabin,The mosaics of Roman North Africa,
    Oxford 1978,176 ff.

25) Trier,Diözesanmuseum.

26) W.Noll,L.Born und R.Holm,Kölner Jb.13,1972/73,77 ff.

27) D.Baatz,wie Anm.2o,besonders 43 und Anm.13 und 14.
    Untersuchungen E.Denningers,Institut für Technologie
    der Malerei an der Staatl.Akademie der Bildenden Künste,
    Stuttgart.

28) Hölstein und Münsingen: R.Giovanoli,Jahrb.Schweiz.Ges.
    Urgesch.53,1966/67,79 ff;Trier: R.Wihr,Trierer Zeit=
    schrift 29,1966,222 ff; ders.Arbeitsbl.f.Restauratoren
    1,1968,Gr.7,1 ff;Augsburg und Kempten: A.Eibner,Ent=
    wicklung und Werkstoffe der Wandmalerei vom Altertum
    bis zur Neuzeit,München 1926,3o1-3o8; Elst: E.A.Th.
    Bogaers,De gallo-romeinse Tempels te Elst in de Over-
    Betuve,S'Gravenhage 1955,1o4-124.Die Untersuchungen
    führten S.Sneyers,Laboratoire Central des Musees de
    Belgique,Bruxelles 1953 und S.Liberti,Instituto Centra=
    le del Restauro,Rom durch.

29) Köln-Müngersdorf:J.Klinkenberg und K.Würth wie in Anm.5;
    Rom:Vgl.Boll.dell'Istituto Centrale del Restauro,Rom,
    19/2o,1955,1o7;29/3o,1957,37-4o; 1967,7 ff.

3o) F.Müller-Skjold, Über die Technik der antiken Wand=
    malereien und Mosaiken,Ber.VI.Int.Kongreß f.Archäologie,
    Berlin 1939,157-161,bes.16o;ders.Eine Reihenuntersu=
    chung an antiken italischen Marmorstucken,Arch.Anz.
    65/66,195o/51,Sp.132-14o.

31) Wie Anm.26.

32) W.Klinkert,Bemerkungen zur Technik der pompeianischen
Wanddekoration,Röm.Mitt.64,1957 ,111-148.

33) L.u.P.Mora,P.Phillipot,La Conservation des Peintures
murales,Bologna 1977,bes.116/117 u.Anm.55; vgl.auch
P.Mora,Boll.dell'Istituto Centrale del Restauro,Rom
1967,63-84.

34) Salze und Zubereitungen der Kieselfluorwasserstoffsäure.
Die durch Laosin B mit Kalk oder Zement gebildeten Kalk-
Fluor-Verbindungen sind wasserunlöslich.Inzwischen
haben sich zur Verkieselung von archäologischen Objekten
Tegovakon (Goldschmitt,Düsseldorf) oder Funkosil (Wacker,
München)besser bewährt.

35) Mineral;Verwitterungsprodukt verschiedener Glimmerarten;
grüne oder goldbraune,metallisierende,schuppige und
großblättrige Aggregate,monoklin.

36) Die gesundheitsschädigende Wirkung des Lösemittels be=
dingt,daß diese Arbeiten im Freien ausgeführt werden
müssen,wenn keine ausreichenden Absauganlagen und Luft=
zufuhr in den Arbeitsräumen vorhanden sind.

6. WALL PLASTER FROM THE YORK MINSTER EXCAVATIONS, 1967-1973

Brenda Heywood

The excavations beneath York Minster, undertaken during a pro-
gramme of engineering work designed to save the Minster from collapse
and ultimately extended to areas immediately outside the church, revealed the north-west corner of the *principia* of the Roman fortress
and parts of residential buildings in an area usually allotted to the
first cohort of the legion. A wealth of Roman wall-plaster was discovered. It came from three types of structure: plaster rendering from
timber and wattle partitions still *in situ*; plaster from partitions
originally based on clay and cobble footings and less frequently
preserved; finally, plaster from stone walls, sometimes still adhering,
sometimes fallen.

Of the first category, four substantial sections of plaster
remained in position, three of which were from the residential buildings, one from the *principia*. Two belonged to a single partition which
probably stood from the early second century into the fourth century
and had been re-rendered several times: one section exhibited no less
than six surfaces, the other no less than five. The plaster coat was
usually white, sometimes decorated simply with red painted lines, but
one rendering was of a richly coloured design in black, blue and red.
One portion of this partition (4 ft. 9 ins. x 2 ft. 10 ins. x 9 ins.;
1.45 m. x 0.86 m. x 0.23m.), conserved by Norman Davey, is now on
display in the Undercroft of York Minster. From the second category,
only small fragments of plaster remained *in situ*. It is clear, however,
that both types of plaster partition were demolished later in the Roman
period and levelled to form floor bases for presumably the same rooms.
The vast bulk of wall-plaster from the excavations was found re-used in
this way and clearly it will be a painstaking task to reconstruct the
original designs, if any, which once adorned the partitions.

Of the final category two notable examples survive: firstly a
slab of plaster from the fallen clerestorey of the *principia*, not yet
studied; secondly, the already well-known painted wall-plaster recovered
from a fourth-century annexe to the north-west side of the basilica. A
large area of the latter has been reconstructed by Norman Davey and re-
erected in the Undercroft, close to the Roman annexe wall from which it
fell (approx. 17 ft. x 11 ft.; 5.18 m. x 3.35 m.). It shows a threefold
horizontal division, a marbled dado, a central field subdivided into
panels, and a frieze with the outline of a window framed by the
surviving plaster (Fig.6.1).

The detailed study of the decoration of the wall-plaster must
await the definitive report on the Roman buildings in Volume I of
the York Minster Excavations. Although of no great artistic merit, its
considerable interest and importance lie in the fact that it is from
a military rather than a civilian context.

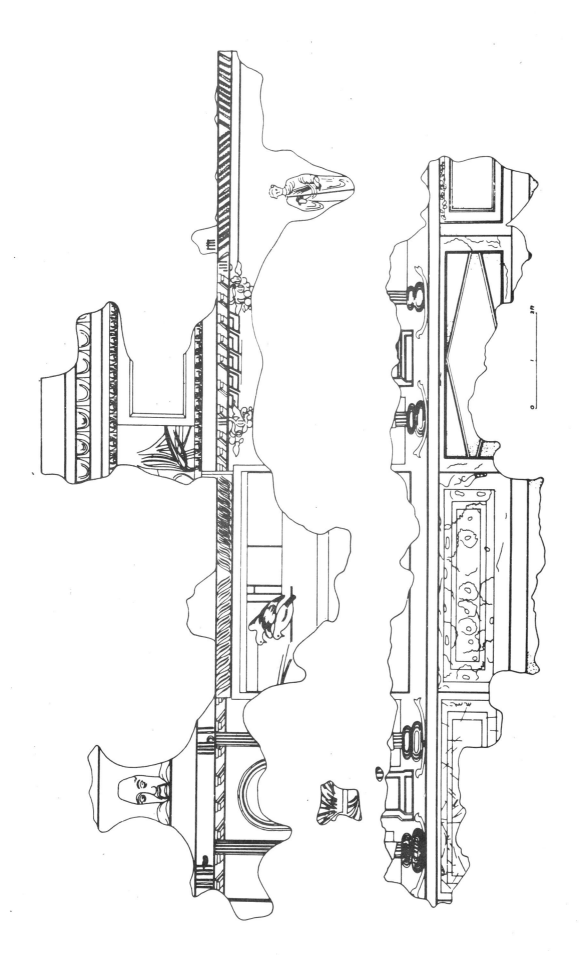

Fig. 6.1: York, 4th cent. plaster found under the Minster (N. Davey).

7. THE KINGSCOTE WALL-PAINTINGS

Roger Ling

The paintings discussed were discovered during excavations in 1976 by the Kingscote Archaeological Association, directed by E.J. Swain. They had collapsed concertina fashion above the Venus mosaic pavement in a small hypocausted room at the western extremity of the main building excavated at Kingscote (Gloucestershire). Most of the fragments were lifted and patiently reconstructed by Dr. Norman Davey, who produced five largish areas of a figured fresco, over two-thirds life-size, which was attributed to the room's south wall. Dated by the excavators to the late third or early fourth century, the most extensive element reconstructed shows a pair of seated figures bracketing a Cupid who flies towards the right-hand figure. Above the Cupid are the remains of three female figures with nimbed heads. Other elements are part of a figure perhaps reclining on its left elbow with a reed in the hand, and part of a seated figure with a calathus of flowers beside it (fig. 7.1).

Although the fragmentary state of the paintings makes interpretation difficult, the presence of Cupid implies a Greek mythological love-scene. The right-hand seated figure has the long drapery of a female, and a shield rests at its side; but the left leg is exposed in a way quite inappropriate for a martial deity like Minerva or Dea Roma. Another possibility is Achilles disguised as a woman among the daughters of Lycomedes on the island of Scyros. Normally Achilles would not be shown seated after he received the arms which lured him to reveal himself; but a sarcophagus from Crete in the British Museum shows a version of the scene where the hero already has the arms but still lingers on his throne, as though reluctant to go to war. Alternatively, by analogy with a scene on fourth-century B.C. Scythian bow-cases, we may have a leave-taking between Achilles and Lycomedes' family which takes place after he has been revealed. In either case the Cupid would refer to the love of Achilles for Deidameia (perhaps the seated figure at the left). The figures with the reed and the calathus may not necessarily belong to the same scene.

A fuller publication of the paintings, written in conjunction with E.J. Swain, will appear elsewhere. (See also brief account *Britannica*, xii (1981), 167-175).

Figure 7.1 : Kingscote Villa (N.Davey)

8. NEW DISCOVERIES FROM THE NORFOLK STREET VILLA, LEICESTER

Jean E. Mellor

This paper is divided into three sections, dealing firstly with
the context from which the wall-paintings were recovered, secondly
with the discovery of the wall-paintings and the problems which their
excavation presented and thirdly, with the wall-paintings themselves.

A word of caution would be appropriate here: it will be apparent
that much of what follows is very much an interim statement. The wall-
paintings themselves are still in the process of reconstruction and
much more research is required when their conservation has been completed. Some possible lines of enquiry are outlined at the end of the
paper.

In addition, very little of the other material from the site has
been studied in any detail and further excavation, which began in
October 1980, will doubtless necessitate the revision of some of the
statements made below.

1. The villa lies about half a mile outside the Roman town of Ratae
    Coritanorum, on rising ground west of the river Soar. The site
    has been known since the late 18th century when pavements were
    noted during grubbing out operations in the Cherry Orchard there
    (Nichols I (1)12). In 1851 the Leicester Literary and Philosophical
    Society uncovered a series of tessellated pavements and in the
    following year the apsidal, dolphin mosaic was lifted and removed
    to the, then, City Museum. The plan of the 1851 excavations showed
    a single range of rooms opening off a corridor on the east side
    while the existence of a north wing was indicated by a second
    corridor pavement at right angles to the first. (See fig.8.1).
    In 1868 the existence of this north wing was apparently confirmed
    when a further fragment of pavement was recorded during the build-
    ing of terrace houses on the south side of Watts Causeway (now
    King Richard's Road).

    In 1975 excavations by the Leicestershire Archaeological Field Unit
    on the east side of Norfolk Street revealed an open courtyard
    area with an aisled barn or workshop to the south,[1] but it was not
    until 1979 that excavation was possible on the site of the presumed
    north wing. Between February and May 1979 a range of rooms was
    uncovered in this area with a separate block at the north-east
    corner, probably a bath-house, with hypocausts and tessellated
    floors. It was to this block that the pavement recorded in 1868
    belonged.

    From the 1975 and 1979 excavations it became clear that the 19th
    century discoveries represented a late stage in the development of
    the site which had been occupied since the mid-second century at
    least. This earlier occupation was represented mainly by a series
    of channels and gullies running down the slope and by a number of

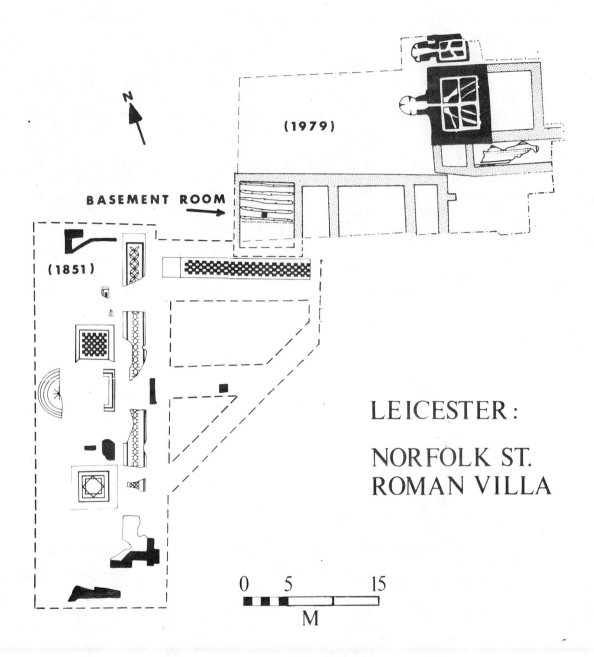

N

(1979)

BASEMENT ROOM

(1851)

LEICESTER:

NORFOLK ST.
ROMAN VILLA

0   5   15

M

Figure 8.1 : Plan of main villa buildings recovered in 1851 and 1979

hearths or ovens of varying shapes and sizes. There were a
few other structures indicated by slight stone foundations
but a dwelling house associated with this phase of activity
has not been identified.

Major re-organisation of the site seems to have taken place in
the late 3rd century with the construction of at least some of
the stone buildings. In its latest phase the complex, as it is
known so far, consisted of a series of buildings ranged round
three sides of an open area or courtyard.

The west wing consisted of a range of rooms, the central one of
which was apsidal, opening off a corridor. Initially, some of
these rooms had floors of mortar or opus signinum which were
later replaced by tessellated pavements. Most of these had very
simple geometric patterns, carried out in coarse red and grey
tesserae. South of the courtyard, which had a rather patchy
mortar surface, was a large aisled barn or workshop built mainly
of timber.

The plan of the main north wing was apparently very simple,
comprising a single range of rooms opening off a corridor on
the south. Of the known rooms in this range only the corridor
seems to have had a tessellated pavement; in the rooms at the
east end of the block only traces of thin mortar floors on clay
foundations survived.

At the north-east corner of this wing was a separate block with
its own corridor off which led another series of rooms. All the
rooms excavated in this block had tessellated floors similar in
design and construction to those of the west wing. Two of the
rooms had channelled hypocausts and in the larger of these the
openings of wall flues survived.

The wall-paintings however, were associated with the west end of
the main north wing. Here two adjacent rooms on the ground floor
had walls decorated in contrasting styles while a cellar or basement room below also had painted walls but with very simple geometric patterns.

All the buildings were of substantial construction with stone
foundations and tiled roofs. The general impression is of solid
comfort with some refinement in the form of tessellated floors
and decorated walls though without achieving the height of elegance
or sophistication. It is in this context that the wall-paintings
should be seen.

2. Towards the west end of the north wing a cellar of Roman date was
   identified which had apparently gone out of use and filled up
   with rubble after which the stone from the cellar walls had been
   robbed. Consequently work in this area began with the excavation
   of the robber trenches. Very little material had been removed from
   the robber trench of the east cellar wall, however, before it
   became apparent that, although the stonework had been robbed, the
   plaster facing here still remained in position as a thin vertical
   sheet held between the filling of the robber trench and the rubble
   filling of the cellar. Although only the back of the plaster was

Plate 8.1 : Painted plaster fragments from west side of
clay-brick wall, as found in cellar filling.

visible at this stage the possibility of wall-paintings on the face could not be ignored so the usual sequence of operations was reversed and the excavation of the rubble filling of the cellar was begun.

When about 1 m. of the rubble had been removed, large fragments of painted plaster were exposed, lying face upwards and forming a fairly coherent layer (see pl. 8.1). The fragments were lifted and removed to the Museum laboratory.

Immediately below this layer of plaster was the collapsed wall itself which had been constructed of unbaked clay bricks bonded together with more clay. It was evidently a partition wall from the ground floor, between the room above the cellar and that to the west and, during the process of decay or demolition, it had collapsed, more or less intact into the cellar beneath (see pl. 8.2). Below the wall, lying face downwards, was the plaster from its east face, appearing as a continuous sheet covering an area of c.15 sq.m. This was lifted in small sections and removed to the laboratory for conservation and reconstruction. (For an account of this process see below p.141).

When the excavation of the cellar was complete, large areas of painted wall-plaster were revealed, still in position on the east and west walls, despite the robbing of the stonework. Two layers of plaster were present on each wall. Moreover, not only did the basement room have painted walls but evidence for a substantial floor was indicated by trenches for joists and a rectangular stone base for some feature was also found in position.

3. Two phases of decoration were represented by the wall-plaster on the walls of the basement room. In both phases the decoration consisted of simple geometric designs carried out in a restricted range of colours on a white background above a wide blue-grey dado. In phase 1 on the west wall rectangles were outlined in broad red and narrow black lines while on the opposite wall in the same phase the main design was composed of broad red vertical and diagonal lines forming a trellis-like pattern. On each wall this layer of wall-plaster had been systematically pecked to provide a key for the next layer. In the second phase the decoration was similar on both walls; rectangular panels were outlined in broad red and yellow lines on a white background.

Despite the simplicity of design here there are one or two points of interest to be noted, in particular perhaps, the use of different patterns on the opposing walls in the earlier phase. However, as no plaster survived on the north wall and the south wall lay outside the limits of the excavation, any further speculation about the overall appearance of the room at this time is unprofitable.

The wall-paintings from the two adjacent rooms on the ground floor provide a striking contrast in style both with each other and with the basement room. That from the room to the west (i.e., the fragments found lying face upwards above the collapsed wall in the cellar filling) was less complete and reconstruction work had only just begun when it had to be suspended in order to deal with the larger section. However, it has so far been possible to reconstruct

Plate 8.2 : East-west section through cellar filling, showing
collapsed partition wall from ground floor.

an area c. 2m. x 1m. Here the most striking feature of the decoration was a horizontal frieze or garland of green leaves with yellow
fruits, perhaps peaches or oranges, painted on a white ground.
Above this are panels outlined in shaded red, yellow and possibly
green, with pyramids of three red spots at the corners. The horizontal garland appears to occupy a position near the top of
the decoration. It is perhaps worth noting here that if this
material had been found first as isolated fragments it would not
have been possible to tell whether the garland was vertical or
horizontal; this was only apparent from the relationship of the
fragments to the clay-brick wall beneath them. The general
impression of the decoration here, from the small panel reconstructed so far is pleasantly light and delicate.

The adjacent room, immediately above the cellar was decorated in
a quite different style. The section recovered from below the clay-
brick wall, is largely complete and represents the entire decorative scheme from floor to ceiling and more than half the length
of the wall.

The main zone of decoration is composed of alternate large panels
of red and green, separated by illusionistic columns, entwined
with vine scrolls and with Corinthian-type capitals, all below an
imitation ovolo with a further, floral, frieze above this. The
section which has been recovered consists of two complete red
panels, one complete green one and part of another. Below this
zone is a pale yellow band and then a series of smaller panels
alternately long and short, painted in imitation marbling above a
splashed pink baseboard, (Fig.7.2).

The large red panels have a pair of white inner border lines and
are framed with a band of darker red with a blue band round that.
The corresponding elements of the green panels are respectively
yellow, white and red.

From the top corners of the red panels hangs a green garland. No
attempt has been made to render this realistically; it is painted
in small green blotches very close together with occasional high-
lights in white and yellow.

Within the complete green field is a small picture panel in a wide
yellow frame. The design within the frame is unfortunately very
fragmentary but what is left does suggest a picture, perhaps a
landscape, with some unidentified object in the foreground. The
upper part is painted in pale blue shading into greens and browns
at the bottom while just off centre is a swirling mixture of deep
pink and white with an indication of something else which might
conceivably be a raised sword. There seems little doubt that the
intention was to represent an actual picture in a wooden frame;
a wooden frame of identical type and similar dimensions is in the
British Museum.[2]

The fact that so much of this central motif is missing suggests
the possibility that it had been damaged or deliberately defaced
before the wall collapsed.

Between the large panels are illusionistic columns, the shafts

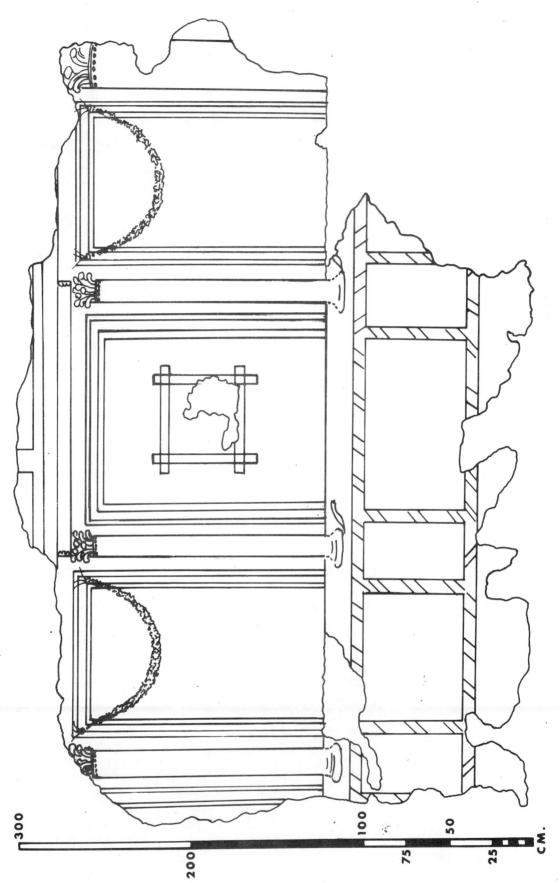

Figure 8.2 : Decorative scheme of main section of wall-plaster

painted in greyish pinks and purples, with yellow capitals and yellow and brown bases. To the right of each of the surviving bases is a green leaf-shaped object, probably an attempt at a shadow. Round the column shafts spiral white vine scrolls which, in contrast to the green garlands, are painted realistically, (pl. 8.3).

There seems to have been an attempt in this zone of decoration to suggest volume and perspective but the result is rather confused. The light seems to be coming from within the red panels rather than from a single external source, though the 'shadows' at the bases of the columns fall consistently to the right.

Above the large panels is a large scale imitation ovolo painted in pink and greyish purple on a white ground and above this, though rather fragmentary, is a frieze of white, yellow and green leaves on a dark red background.

The long and short marbled panels on the lower part of the wall echo the arrangement of the main zone with the narrow panels coming below the columns. The narrow panels are painted in somewhat darker shades than the long ones, being alternately green and grey with white scribbles and grey with green, blue and yellow blobs. The long panels below the red fields have green, blue and yellow streaks and blobs on a white ground all overlain by red scribbles. Those below the green fields have a yellow ground with red and white streaks and blobs again overlain by red scribbles. All the panels are framed by green and white streaked bands.

It seems likely that the original height of the room was something in excess of 3.00 m. the maximum height of the surviving section being 2.97 m. The splashed pink baseboard is incomplete and ragged but at one point at least the full depth appears to be represented where the painting is overlain by splashes of coarse pink mortar, which presumably indicate the junction with the floor. The full width of the floral frieze above the ovolo at the top of the section however is not represented.

It is possible to make an estimate of the total length of the wall. The salvaged section is c. 4.50 m. long and includes three complete panels and part of a fourth with the intervening columns, see fig. 8.2. The column at the right (i.e. north) end of the section is very much wider than the rest and presumably marks the end of the original wall. If the design is reconstructed with five complete panels and another broad column at the south end the total length would be 7.20 m. A room of this size here would fit reasonably well with the position of the east-west corridor recorded in 1851, although the accuracy of the 19th century plan leaves something to be desired. However, if the room with the wall painting is assumed to be the same size as the basement below then the rectangular stone base recorded in the latter would occupy the central position.

The quality of the finished surface varied in different areas of the wall painting, and it is not always easy to distinguish to what extent these variations are due to conditions of burial or to what extent they reflect the original techniques or the survival qualities of the pigments. In some areas it is clear that the paint

Plate 8.3 : Detail of painted vine scroll round one of the
columns on the main section of wall-painting.
The join between applications of plaster can be
seen on the left.

was applied to a rougher plaster surface, for example in places the pink baseboard has a much coarser texture, especially towards the bottom. Over most of the wall the surface is good though un-remarkable, but one of the red panels retains an exceptionally smooth almost polished surface while the other, by contrast, is extremely patchy and has lost a good deal of the colour. Here the loss of colour seems to be at least partly the result of an accident of burial as this area has been compressed onto a layer of very sticky clay which, when it was removed during the cleaning process brought the paint off too.

This suggests that a true fresco technique was not used here but this question still requires further investigation, as does the polished surface of the other red panel.

What appears to be an example of careless workmanship can be seen in the green and white streaked bands surrounding the marbled panels where there is occasional but inconsistent variation in the direction of the streaks.

The application of the wall-plaster was carried out in two quite separate stages and the painting of the first stage was completed before the second layer was applied. Evidence for this was first observed while the plaster was still in the ground when distinct differences in the colour of the plaster backing could be seen. Now that the work of re-assembly is complete the joints or seams between the two applications of plaster can be traced clearly on the face of the wall-painting, see fig. 8.3.

The plaster base for the red panels, including the columns, the ovolo and the frieze, was applied first and this area was painted. Not only was the basic colour applied but some, if not all, of the decorative detail was completed before the second layer of plaster, the green panels and the lower part of the wall, was applied. This can be seen clearly at the sides of the green panels, where the second layer of plaster overlaps the columns and covers the overpainted white vine scrolls.

The recovery, not only of such a large and relatively complete section of wall-painting but also of the decoration from the adjacent room from the basement below provides us with a unique opportunity to study not only a variety of styles of decoration from the same building but also to investigate some of the methods and techniques which were employed. It must be clear from the preceeding account that there are a number of questions demanding further investigation and various lines of research can be proposed.

Some of these have already been mentioned above, for example the question of whether a true fresco technique was employed. The evidence at present seems conflicting; the application of two distinct layers of plaster suggests a fresco technique whereas the flaking off of the paint from some areas indicates that a bond between plaster and paint was not achieved.

Analysis of the pigments has already begun though no results are available yet. It is intended to compare the pigments used in the three rooms to see if, for example, cheaper, or more easily

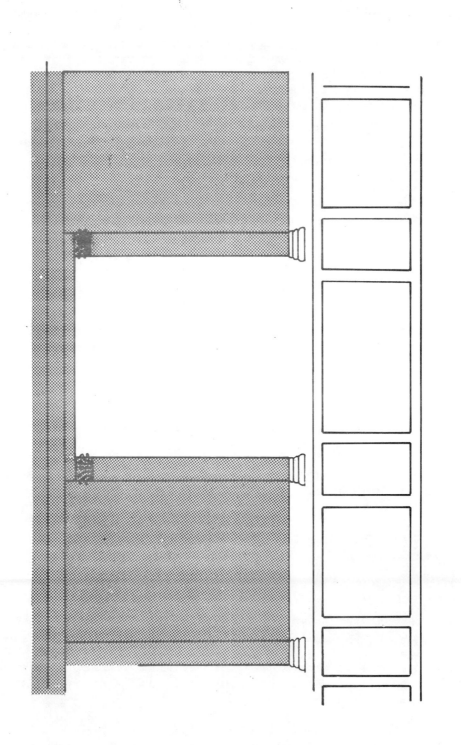

FIRST APPLICATION OF WALLPLASTER

Figure 8.3 : Diagram illustrating method of application

138

available colours were used in the basement. It may additionally be possible to identify the medium used for the overpainting and decorative detail, at least to indicate whether it was organic or inorganic. It is also proposed to examine the plaster itself, its constituents and their relative proportions. The use of marble powder is suggested as contributory to the very smooth polished surface of some areas and it should be possible to identify this material if it is present.

The exact date of the wall-paintings has yet to be established. Comparatively little dating evidence was recovered from the excavations and the significance of the material has yet to be assessed. The tessellated pavements are 4th century in style and a coin of the first half of the 4th century was found in the rubble filling of the stoke-hole of the larger hypocaust. It is not impossible, however, that the main north wing was the first of this series of buildings to be constructed, and that the wall-paintings belong to an earlier phase than the tessellated pavements. Once again, further work remains to be done.

The paintings from the Norfolk Street villa are not the only examples of such decoration from Leicester. In 1958 Mr.Wacher recovered fine examples of paintings from the walls and a ceiling of a house of second century date within the town.[3] Comparison of the styles, material and techniques used in interior decoration in a town house and a villa in the same area though of different dates should prove fruitful. Finally the wall-paintings must also be seen in the context in which they were found, in association with the other evidence of the buildings, their construction, function, comfort or otherwise and their embellishment and in this way to help to clarify the picture of the life-style of the inhabitants of a modest villa on the outskirts of a provincial Roman town.

ACKNOWLEDGEMENTS

I should like to thank Dr. Roger Ling for his continuing interest in and comments on the wall-paintings from Leicester.

NOTES

1. Britannia VII, p975 Pl. XXVIIB.

2. Hinks, 1933 pl. xxiv. I am indebted to Dr.D.J. Smith for bringing this reference to my attention.

3. Davey, 1972:262

BIBLIOGRAPHY

Britannia, 1976. VII.

Davey, N., 1972. 'Conservation of Romano-British Painted Plaster 251-265', *Britannia III*.

Hinks, R.P., 1933. *Catalogue of the Greek, Etruscan and Roman Paintings and Mosaics in the British Museum*.

Nichols, J., 1795-1811. *The History and Antiquities of the County of Leicester*. 8 vols.

9. THE LIFTING OF THE ROMAN WALLPLASTER
FROM THE NORFOLK STREET ROMAN VILLA, LEICESTER, ENGLAND

Theodore Sturge

Introduction

The purpose of this paper is to describe the lifting and recording of the fallen wallplaster from the cellar of the Norfolk Street
Roman Villa in Leicester, England. The work will be described in detail
so that it can be used as a guide should others encounter similar
problems. For details of how it was found, reference should be made to
Jean Mellor's paper in this volume of B.A.R. The material was in two
distinct categories, the face up material and the face down material.
As the problems were quite different, they will be dealt with separately.

The Face Up Material

When the wall fell, the shock made the plaster break away from
the wall and scatter. However, although the pieces became in some cases
considerably separated, they retained their approximate relative
positions. Before it was lifted the plaster was washed sufficiently
for it to be drawn and photographed in situ. Care must be taken if
using bowls of water and sponges as they rapidly become dirty and the
dirt then acts as an unwelcome abrasive. Care must also be taken
because the pigments may be water soluble.

The fragments were lifted by sliding knives and trowels under
them to free them. The fragments were then placed on boards as nearly
as possible in the position they were found in. No attempt was made at
this stage to reposition pieces, partly to save time but also because
of the danger of making a mistake which would make later work in the
laboratory more difficult. One red line looks much like another at
this stage when the material is only partly clean. A plan was made to
show where the boards of pieces fitted relative to one another.

The Face Down Material

This was rather a different problem because it involved working
from the back of plaster without knowing what was on the face. The
plaster appeared as a fairly solid unbroken sheet. For this reason,
the initial attempt at lifting was very simple. A small section was
freed from the main body of plaster by cutting with a saw right
through to the rubble underneath. Trowels were then pushed underneath
to remove the section. However, as soon as this was tried it was found
to be totally impractical. This was because the plaster was in two
distinct layers. The backing plaster, which was 30-40 mm. thick and
fairly soft, had bent to the shape of the rubble fill when it fell.
However, the fine layer of painted plaster was harder and more brittle
and rather than bend had shattered on impact.

At some stage the cellar was flooded and this resulted in a silt like mud being carried into all the cracks between the pieces of fine plaster. This also, in parts, got right between the fine and the rough layers of plaster. Parts of the fill in the cellar were muddy in nature while others were sandy. This affected both the preservation of the plaster and the lifting. Those areas lying on a well drained sandy layer were in excellent condition but those on a muddy layer were in less good condition. The areas of plaster lying on mud appeared to have had the lime leeched out of them, reducing the strength of the plaster and the bond of the paint layer. In the worst area on the right hand red panel, the paint was, in part, separated from the remaining plaster by a layer of mud and the edges of the fragments were badly deteriorated, giving bad joins. The areas lying on sandy material were much easier to undercut during lifting than those areas on mud since the sandy material crumbled easily away.

The second attempt to lift the plaster was made using polyurethane foam. This failed because it was very cold and the plaster was damp. This prevented the foam from forming satisfactorily. Also, had it been used, it would have given considerable problems in the laboratory when we came to remove it because the gas which forms the bubbles is extremely toxic and is released when the foam is cut.

Finally, the traditional method using plaster of paris was used. This process will be described stage by stage:

1. First the rough backing plaster was removed (see fig. 9.1). This was done for two reasons: a) to reduce the weight of the lifted sections and b) as has already been noted, the fine plaster layer was very poorly attached to the rough plaster, so it tended to drop off during lifting. The rough plaster was soft and easily removed with trowels. The back of the fine plaster was clearly defined by a change from soft to hard. Also, some areas had a layer of mud between the two layers. This mud was, as far as possible, scraped off as it prevented the plaster of paris sticking. The remaining layer of fine plaster varied from about 5-25 mm. in thickness.

2. Next, plaster of paris (bought in bulk and mixed in a rubber bucket) was applied to an area of about 1.5 m². The plaster of paris was poured on to the back of the plaster and spread, with trowels, to a thickness of about 4 mm. While the plaster of paris was still wet, cloth was spread out and pressed into the surface. Initially, plasterer's scrim was used. However, in the later stages large pieces of hessian were used instead. On top of the cloth a second layer of plaster of paris was applied to give a total thickness of 6-10 mm. One problem with plaster of paris is that it expands as it sets and on a large area this can make it bow and lift away from the Roman plaster. This problem is overcome by applying the plaster of paris to small areas, allowing it to set and then joining the small areas together with more plaster of paris.

3. It was not possible to lift very large areas at once so the plaster of paris had to be divided, with a saw, into sections about 250 x 400 mm. A curved floorboard saw (fig. 9.1) is ideal for this since it is designed to cut into a flat surface. Not all floorboard saws are curved quite like this one: the one we used was made by Tyzack. It should be noted that using a saw for this purpose completely

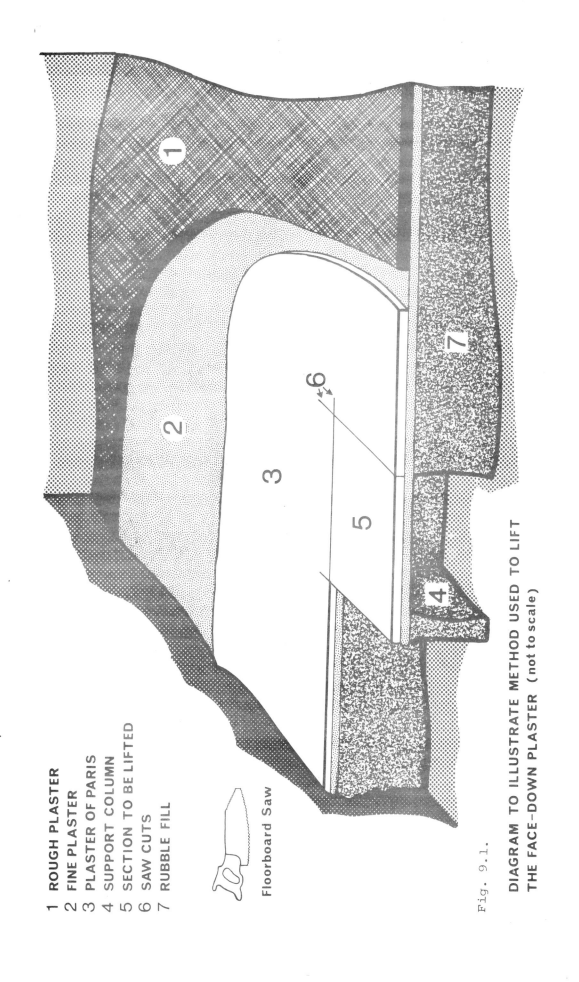

1 ROUGH PLASTER
2 FINE PLASTER
3 PLASTER OF PARIS
4 SUPPORT COLUMN
5 SECTION TO BE LIFTED
6 SAW CUTS
7 RUBBLE FILL

Floorboard Saw

Fig. 9.1.

DIAGRAM TO ILLUSTRATE METHOD USED TO LIFT
THE FACE-DOWN PLASTER (not to scale)

143

ruins it, so one should be purchased specially. The cut (see fig. 9.1) went right through the plaster of paris but not the Roman plaster. There is no problem stopping at this point as the feel and sound change once the Roman plaster is reached. At this stage the sections are numbered with a very large felt tip pen and their positions marked on a plan. Also, the edges are marked so that they correspond with those of the pieces next to them so that they can be laid out the right way round in the laboratory. All markings on the plaster of paris must be very bold otherwise they are easily rubbed off.

4. Each section was undercut individually using trowels, knives and fingers. The plaster of paris did not stick very well to the Roman plaster, partly because of residual mud and partly because it was very wet (it was impossible to dry it out). This was a mixed blessing. It meant that it was very easy to separate the Roman material in the laboratory but it tended to drop off during lifting. Usually the plaster was connected to the main body of plaster on two sides. This left one corner with no support. For this reason, during undercutting a column was left at the end not attached to the main body (see fig. 9.1) to take the weight while the rest was undercut. When the rest was free this column was gradually removed and a board the same size as the section was slid into place on the face of the Roman plaster to hold the pieces in place against the plaster of paris. This sandwich of plywood/Roman plaster/ plaster of paris could then be wriggled free from the main body of plaster. The Roman plaster separated along pre-existing breaks. This sandwich can then be turned over to leave the Roman plaster lying on its plaster of paris support. This is best done over a clean board so that any pieces that fall out can be easily retrieved.

5. The lifted sections were then taken to the laboratory and laid out. It was found that if the plaster was allowed to dry out before it was cleaned, the mud or clay on the surface shrank and tended to pull the pigment off with it. For this reason it was kept wet by regular spraying and keeping it under polythene sheet. Storage in damp conditions, however, tended to give mould growth so a small amount of sodium ortho phenyl phenate was added to the spray water as a mould inhibitor. A protective mask must be worn during spraying if fungicide is used.

10. ROMANO-BRITISH WALL-PAINTINGS FROM TARRANT HINTON, DORSET

Lt-Col. G.E. Gray

1" OS sheet 179 or 1:50,000 sheet 195. ST927118.

1. 7 km NE of BLANDFORD FORUM: 1 km W of R road BADBURY RINGS to
    KINGSTON DEVERELL and probably BATH (Margary 46); 7 km W of R
    road BADBURY RINGS to OLD SARUM (Margary 4c).

2. The site was investigated following agricultural operations in
    1845 when crops withered during drought. The report referred to
    walls "with stucco and coloured facings" also "walls three feet
    in thickness, with a smooth plaster on the interior surface, on
    which appeared frescoes of various patterns, representing ribbon
    work, arches, foliage, &c probably, from their situation, borders
    to more elaborate central designs". The report continued with the
    suggestion that "the remains indicate that a Roman village, or
    small town, stood upon the spot, the name of which is now buried
    in oblivion".[1]

3. No plan of the excavation was then made therefore the exact location
    cannot be identified but a scatter of pottery etc. within Barton
    Field suggested a site and trial trenches were excavated in 1968.
    These yielded amongst other materials, some painted wall-plaster.

4. Extensive excavation during subsequent summers yielded quantities
    of wall-plaster from three separate rooms, viz., Building II Room I,
    Building II Room II and Building III Room I.[2] Only the first of
    these has yet been studied and reconstruction is now well advanced.
    Three qualities of plaster have been noted -

    4.1 Very hard sand coloured homogeneous backing up to
         50 mm thick with hard white facing film of plaster
         to which pigment had been applied.

    4.2 Much softer backing with pieces of chalk up to
         5 mm cube and some evidence of having been applied
         to wattle; probably an upper floor room or ceiling.
         Paint as applied to surface much thicker and
         consequently less smooth than 4.1 above.

    4.3 Very hard sandy backing similar to 4.1 but bearing
         an extremely hard white very smooth almost polished
         thin facing decorated with pink, green and mauve
         narrow stripes which gave the impression of little
         more than staining the surface. There is positively
         no indication that this effect is due to the wearing
         away of a thicker paint surface.

5. All the qualities of plaster appear to be very durable and fractures have remained sharp. The pigments are well fixed and withstand moderate handling, with the exception of Pompeian red which has little resistance to water. The robustness of the plaster, doubtless due to the chalky nature of the site, compares favourably with fragments from another site some 30 km distant, where there is an acid soil, which are little more than lumps of sand held together by the paint film.

6. It is clear from the excavation that the buildings have been subjected at some time to extensive robbing, as a source of stone, and further were probably part wattle or other non-stone construction so that much of the wall-plaster is unlikely to have survived for recovery. The quantities recovered to date are insufficient to indicate the complete design of any one wall but it has been possible to put together sections of the decorations which it is hoped might be interpreted by art historians to suggest a more complete picture of the villa as it might have looked when occupied.

7. Notable assemblages include:-

7.1 A human foot 230 mm heel to toe and shin up to knee level facing left to right close to a left side vertical border and a similar foot only forward of the first resting on a plinth 285 mm high. (Pl.10.1).

7.2 A spear head pointing downwards ahead of the second foot and further ahead a sword or dagger hilt pointing upwards. (Pl.10.2).

7.3 Both the feet, the spear head and the hilt can be related to the upper edge of a dado design comprising at least two roundels 320 mm diameter each surrounded by a wreath and interspaced by panels of marbling and/or leaf design. (Pl.10.3).

7.4 A human face looking languidly downwards to its right with curly hair[3] and similar hair only without features to the left. The neck and right shoulder of the first face have also been assembled. Over and behind these heads is a satyr-like head with apparently no body but mounted on what might be a fountain base. (Pl.10.4).

7.5 A golden disc 120 mm diameter associated with green clothing folds and a flesh coloured area which could be an elbow and arm from below the shoulder to above the wrist. The golden disc bears a representation of a human face; a second similar but incomplete golden disc has been identified. (Pl.10.5).

7.6 An urn or font like structure of essentially classical form with a gadroon decorated base.

8. All the above assemblages are in the first category described in paragraph 4.1. In the second category, the designs fall mainly into two types, namely, massed fruit and floral decoration of which there are more than 250 fragments yet it has been virtually

Plate 10.1 : Human feet.

Plate 10.2 : Spear head.

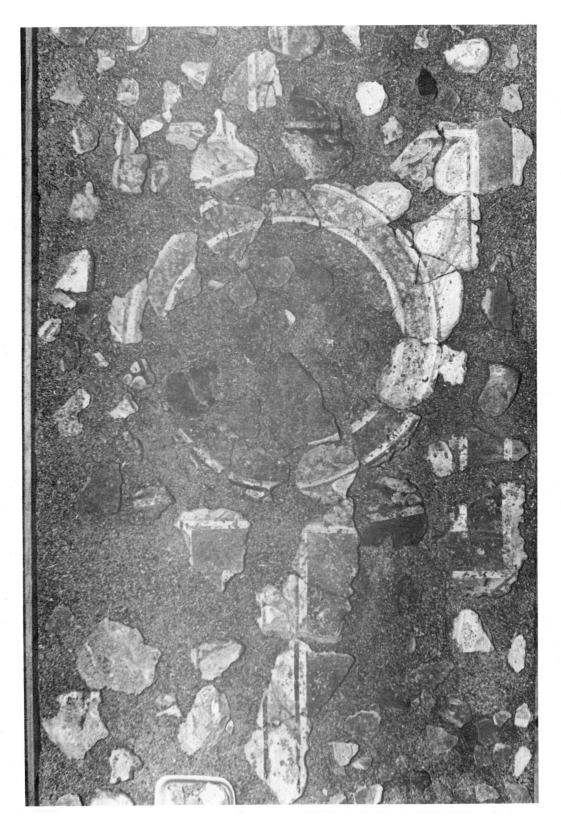

Plate 10.3 : Section of dado.

Plate 10.4 : On left, human face with curly hair.
Above right, ? satyr's head.

Plate 10.5 : Golden disc decorated with human face.

impossible to match adjacent pieces and secondly brightly coloured red, green, yellow, blue grey and mauve banded borders which clearly enclose the floral designs but from which it has not yet been possible to establish overall sizes or to relate them to wall or ceiling sizes.

9. In the same quality of plaster there is an assemblage of connected archways, possibly those referred to in Hutchins, which gives a distinct impression that the artist was trying to indicate a perspective. Other assemblages include spiral geometric patterns in the same vivid colours as the banded borders also some vivid blue colouring incorporating material to provide a glistening effect.

10. Restoration work is still continuing on plaster from Building II Room I and will be followed by work on the other rooms. There is evidence that plaster from Building III Room I includes some from a barrel vaulted ceiling which will present specialised restoration problems.

NOTES

1. J. Hutchins, *History and Antiquities of the County of Dorset* (1845) I:319.

2. Tanner and Giles, "A Guide to the Excavations at Barton Field, Tarrant Hinton, (Wimborne, 1972)"; *Britannia* XI (1980):291-2 with plan, fig.20.

3. Suggested by Dr.R. Ling as Narcissus gazing at his reflection in the water.

11. THE RESTORATION OF THE LULLINGSTONE ROMAN WALL-PLASTER

Frances Weatherhead

This report is intended to give a brief survey of the restoration work so far carried out on the wall-plaster from Lullingstone Roman villa, in Kent. A fuller and more descriptive account will be found in the forthcoming publication, which is well illustrated.[1]

While a considerable amount of work has been carried out over the years since excavation by various individuals, a vast amount of effort and time still needs to be spent joining individual fragments together, linking up design areas, and relating these to various walls. So far only two areas have been completely restored and mounted for exhibition.

The wall-plaster had originally decorated the Christian rooms at Lullingstone, that is the House-Church and the Antechamber situated towards the northern end of the villa. It is dated to the second half of the fourth century. The House-Church was built over the so-called Deep Room, which was used in the third century for pagan cult practices and was itself decorated with wall-paintings. At the end of the fourth century or the beginning of the fifth, a fire occurred in the villa which caused the walls of the House-Church to collapse and the wall-paintings which covered them to break up and fragment into small pieces. The whole structure fell into the Deep Room below, thus forming a confused mass of debris.

The villa was excavated by Col. Meates from 1949 to 1957. While excavating the debris that filled the Deep Room the excavators noticed that the edges of the fragments of wall-plaster from the upper room were in fact quite well preserved and some of these fragments could be joined. It was decided to collect the plaster and to see what designs could be produced by piecing it together. (However, some of the plainer areas *were* thrown away.) Plaster was also collected from the Antechamber, the room to the north which led into the House-Church, with the intention of reconstruction. This was to be the first major restoration project of its kind in Britain.

In the early 1950s Mr. Cragoe Nicholson and other early workers managed to piece certain areas together and to work out roughly from which walls various areas of plaster had fallen. An artist's drawing from this time shows what was believed to have decorated the West wall and part of the South wall of the House-Church, while another shows a design believed to have decorated the South wall of the Antechamber.[2] On the West wall were six figures, separated by columns, their arms outstretched in the *orans* position. Underneath was a dado showing a stylised marble design, which was believed to continue on the East and South walls. (From study of the archaeological evidence, it was thought that the North-wall decoration had been completely destroyed in the fall). On the South wall had been a sacred Chi-Rho monogram surrounded by a

wreath and situated between two columns.[3] From the Antechamber there
had been another Chi-Rho monogram set within a wreath, this time thought
to be bordered top and bottom by a zig-zag design. It thus seemed
evident from these iconographical remains alone that these two rooms had
indeed been used by Christians, possibly even for religious ceremonies
but here the wall-paintings can give us no definite evidence.

The wall-plaster from the House-Church and Antechamber was
acquired by the British Museum in 1967, and conservators in the Pre-
historic and Romano-British Department worked further at piecing certain
areas together. The Chi-Rho panel from the South wall of the House-Church
was finally mounted using a method devised by Mr. Peter Shorer, and now
is to be seen in the Romano-British gallery. The second figure from the
West wall was also mounted. A *parapetasmata* or curtain passes behind
him showing that he has passed into the afterlife. In 1973 Dr. Davey
re-restored the West wall, this time including most of the fragments in
order to make up all six figures. This restoration is also exhibited
in the Romano-British gallery. All six figures are thought to show
deceased persons, although it is of course not known who they represent.
The figures wear elaborate robes, crossed by sashes decorated with
pearls, but it is now thought that these robes should be shorter than
that shown in the reconstruction. Some other details in the reconstruction are also debatable, for instance, it is suggested that the dado
should be lower and another zone of decoration may have occurred above
the figured zone. However, in spite of these points and the fact that
there are large areas missing, the general scheme is believed to be
correct.

From 1973 to 1976 I was engaged part-time in furthering the
restoration work, that is until financial problems at the British
Museum halted the project. Many thousands of fragments and joined-up
pieces had been laid out in sawdust upon tables in an arrangement
inherited from the early restorers. These tables corresponded with
various walls from which the fragments were believed to have fallen.
There were also many hundreds of boxes containing unstudied fragments.
Unfortunately, it was not always possible to investigate why certain
arrangements had been placed in particular places on the tables, since
the collection of the plaster and the early restoration work, both
pioneering tasks at the time, had been rather inadequately documented.

I began by accepting the lay-out which had been worked out before
me, and made joins within the various design areas, occasionally adding
material from boxes. Thus the overall design-areas were increased. I
also set up new working areas by extracting material from various
boxes; small numbered stickers were placed on some of these fragments so
that I could keep track of the most "productive" boxes. Some of the
fragments had been burnt in the fire which made joining work particularly
difficult.

As well as scrutinising the fronts of the fragments for colour
and design, I also had a close look at the backs. The plaster fabric
appeared to fall into distinctive groups based on visual characteristics. It thus seemed evident that different plaster mixes had been
applied to different wall areas, possibly even to whole walls. As
some feature areas on the tables had been placed next to other areas
showing no clear association either by design on the painted surface
or by visual characteristics of the plaster backing, it became evident
that a careful reassessment of these features was necessary. Only in
this way could progress towards further reconstruction be made. I

decided to sort through all the individual fragments and design-areas and to arrange them not only according to their painted design, but also according to their type of plaster backing. This caused a lot of shuffling around of the original lay-out, but it was soon found that a considerable measure of success was achieved in making new joins between fragments and in bringing together hitherto unsuspected areas of design. All the Ante-chamber plaster appeared to be of the same type, and thus presented no difficult sorting problems.

The plaster from the House-Church could be divided into two broad categories; this could be taken to imply that it had been applied to two different types of wall construction. One was of flint and mortar and the other was of wattle and daub. The back surface of plaster from flint-and-mortar walls is uneven due to the irregular shapes of the flints, while plaster from wattle-and-daub walls has a relatively smooth back surface and the primary coat appears to have a high content of brick dust.

The South wall plaster appeared to have fallen from a flint-and-mortar wall. This was attested by study of a large piece of plaster showing part of a column which could be allocated with certainty to the west end of the South wall; the conclusion was based on its painted design, the presence of several fragments with traces of a corner, and the position in which it was found during excavation. This piece and other clearly associated fragments were then used as a model for South wall plaster. By comparing this model with other material many previously unsuspected areas of plaster were shown to belong to the South wall, and equally, many groups of fragments once thought to belong to the South wall were shown to have originated from other walls.

Excavations in 1955-7 had revealed House-Church plaster from the eastern end of the Deep Room. Some features of design were noted in site diaries, including a Chi-Rho and plaster from a splayed niche. These fragments provided me with a model for East wall plaster, and thus were used to check and compare other material. East wall plaster is rather similar to that from the South wall, and again appeared to have fallen from a flint-and-mortar wall.

There remained a large quantity of plaster which had a high proportion of brick-dust in its primary coat of plaster-like material, similar to that of the West wall. It was extracted from boxes of previously unstudied fragments, from general sorting areas, and from South wall and East wall material. Since we can be reasonably confident in attributing particular designs to the East wall and South wall so that their respective areas are approximately accounted for, and we are assured of the scheme on the West wall, it is evident by elimination that this plaster can only have originated from the North wall. On the other hand it should be said that study of the fill in the Deep Room had previously led to the conclusion that plaster had not survived from the North wall. This theory should probably be discounted in light of the new evidence. We can assume that the plaster from the North wall, since it is similar to West wall plaster, must also have fallen from a wattle-and-daub wall.

It was thus possible, after sorting the plaster according to different plaster types, to allocate the various design areas to the North, South and East walls in the House-Church. However, this approach assumes that the type of wall construction was consistent along the length of each wall. So far no fragments of different plaster types have been found to *join* which adds support to this assumption. However, there are three design-areas, in which the two distinct types of plaster fabric occur. One is an interlocking circle design (thought to have originated from the ceiling mainly because of its geometric pattern, but which should perhaps be considered to have originated from part of a wall, if one considers its small coverage); another is the stylised roof design (e.g. on the West wall); and the other is an area showing lilies above part of a river. This could mean that designs *were* repeated on different walls, or that construction did in fact change along the walls and joins are yet to be found between wattle-and-daub type plaster and flint-and-mortar type plaster in these three design-areas and possibly also in other areas. The attempted allocation of various features to different walls perhaps only provides a useful starting point for sorting out the plaster, and later work may well prove that a reappraisal of this approach is necessary.

At the end of the project in 1976 I packed up all the plaster which had been laid out on tables into about fifty wooden trays, measuring 1.2 m by 0.75 m. This gave me another opportunity to check through all the design areas I had previously grouped. Each tray was labelled, photographed, and cards were written describing the contents. At present these trays are in store and are inaccessible.

Conjectural Reconstruction of the Wall-paintings from the House-Church

Regrettably, it was not possible in the time available to work out any design-area from the House-Church sufficiently to mount it for exhibition. A lot more sorting and joining work still needs to be done. However, I have produced some drawings[4] based on my previous research, to give an idea of the designs which decorate the South, East and North walls of the House-Church. Although they are drawn as accurately as possible based on careful measurement, they are *not* intended to show definitively what had decorated each wall. Instead, I hope they will act as a useful guide for future restorers. There follows a brief description of the subject matter allocated to each wall shown on these drawings.

The South wall measures 6.75 m, and study of the fragmented designs allows one to estimate a height of about 3 m. (Incidentally, this is the same height as the Antechamber). A double colonnade, each set composed of four blue and brown striped columns, stands above the dado. The artist had attempted to show perspective; the column widths in each colonnade decrease slightly towards the central space, and the spaces between the columns correspondingly also decrease. In the central area stand two figures, possibly martyrs. They are dressed in knee-length brown robes, and one carries a palm frond. Placed close-by is a basket-like object associated with part of a piece of furniture.

The columns support a blue architrave, upon which, above the left-hand colonnade stands a figure. I have suggested that the Chi-Rho panel, already restored and mounted, had originated above the central space between the two sets of columns because the blue fragments at the base of this panel are similar to the architrave fragments. The brown-end column, previously mentioned, is also placed over the blue architrave at the west end of the wall, and its own brown architrave continues along the wall to run behind the wreath of the Chi-Rho panel. Presumably there is also another brown-end column further along the wall to match the one at the west end. I have suggested a doorway just east of the centre of the wall, which would give the inhabitants of the villa private access to the House-Church. There is no direct archaeological evidence for this, although some voussoirs possibly from a doorway were found towards the eastern end of the Deep Room. I have also suggested a possible window east of this doorway, which would then give light from the verandah situated below the living rooms. The window splays are decorated with multi-coloured stripes, and two panels showing fleur-de-lis designs are placed at either side of the window.[5] Alternatively, this area of design, splays and panels, may have originated from the East wall if the East wall had windows as had previously been supposed. However, the fabric appears more like the material from the South wall than that from the East wall. A small bordered panel has been tentatively placed above the doorway.

The East wall is 4.25 m in length. Its Chi-Rho in a stylised wreath is set within a red-bordered niche, and is placed centrally above the dado. On either side there are possibly three columns, striped blue, or pinkish-brown decorated with rosettes and spirals. Between these columns subject matter includes vegetation and two figures. It is probable that as on the South wall there is a two-tiered arrangement above the dado. In the top zone above a band showing a stylised roof, stand three figures on a pale green background and associated with them is an area showing purple stalk-like structures above what looks like a fire. I have also included in this zone a pink area upon which are painted lilies and part of a river. It is likely that columns divide up the subject-matter in the top zone. However, an alternative scheme for this top register shows, on either side of the pale green area, two windows bordered by striped splays and fleur-de-lis panels.

On the North wall there is good evidence for another double colonnade. The columns are variously decorated red, and striped blue. Between the two sets of columns there is what appears to be a pastoral or paradise scene. There are three figures, one holding a basket on his shoulder, and they are surrounded by exotic-looking fruit, pomegranates and cereals. A lively dog is also included in the scene. Beyond the two sets of columns, on either side, there are more feature areas, one containing vegetation, the other an unidentifiable purple object, while at either end of the wall stands a blue column. The profusion of designs attributable to this wall suggests two tiers above the dado. Against a pink background stand two buildings, over a brown structure which has been interpreted as the architrave supported by the columns beneath. Further along this top zone there is a river-garden scene showing lilies and rushes. Again columns divide up the subject-matter. They are striped either blue or light brown. From the side of one blue column floral sprays emerge; and a strange vegetation motif, containing what looks like peacock-eyes, decorates the side of a light brown column and the side of another column. A striped red architrave rests on the columns in the top zone. It is to be noted that the entrance to the Antechamber occurs at the west end of the North wall. The remaining length is about 5.75 m.

The Restoration of the Wall-Paintings from the Antechamber

After many months' work I finally put together the Chi-Rho and zig-zag fragments from the Antechamber and produced a result very different from what had been expected. Here the Chi-Rho in its wreath is set towards the top of a vertical rectangular panel. The simple design together with the bright colours produces a very striking effect. There is an outer green border and within this at the top and at both sides, between purple and red bands, the small plates of the zig-zag run concertina-fashion. The plates are painted alternately grey, white and yellow, and the angles between them are marked with small fleur-de-lis motifs. The scintillating effect of these zig-zags draws one's attention to the religious symbol. The Chi-Rho monogram, painted red on a white background, has an *alpha* and an *omega* on either side. It is set within the wreath, 1.18 m wide, which is made up of circular bands of red, yellow and grey. This is decorated with purple leaves and brightly coloured berries. It is evident that the artist had used a straight-edge to mark out the monogram and a compass to mark out the wreath before he painted in these designs. There is a stylised swag beneath the wreath and attenuated motifs on either side of it. The area directly beneath the swag is missing; it was probably plain white, in which case it may have been thrown away by the excavators. However, there is some plaster showing stylised plants which may have originated from this area.

There is sufficient reassembled material to show that the design of this panel is indisputable. We can also say that it was about 3 m tall by 2.3 m wide. There is even one area showing a side at right-angles to the painted surface; this must be where the edge of the panel abutted against a wooden structure, possibly a doorway. We do not know for certain from which wall it fell, but it would fit comfort-ably on the South or East wall of the Antechamber. There are only a very few fragments left which belong to this panel, for which joins cannot be found. We can therefore say that the restoration is just about as complete as it will ever be.

Other fragments from the Antechamber were made up to form parts of four panels, which had variously coloured borders. The inside areas were marked out with purple lines which had fleur-de-lis motifs in the corners, but which were otherwise plain. Two panels were interconnected, and three abutted against wooden structures. It is not yet possible to say from which wall or walls these panels fell.

There follows a brief note on the method of mounting the plaster for exhibition. The central area of the Antechamber Chi-Rho panel was mounted using the ingenious method devised by my former colleague Mr. Peter Shorer. The joined-up pieces and the carefully placed unattached pieces were set in hardboard and backed up with a foaming plastic. The great advantage of this method is that the mount is kept as light as possible. The process is also reversible.

A wooden frame strengthened with aluminium struts supported the hardboard section. Holes were cut into the hardboard and the fragments set face down in position. 'Polyfilla' was applied round the edges of the fragments so that the fit was perfect. Polyurethane foam was then poured into the frame and the backing board pressed down on top to enable the foam to expand and fill all the available spaces. The board was then tightly secured. The missing areas of design have yet to be painted in on the front of the mount. Unfortunately, I had no time left to finish this work. The paint-work should be a slightly different tone from the original so that one can easily tell what is original and what is make-up. In actual fact there should not be too much difficulty as the technique allowed the fragments to protrude slightly from the facing board. (Initially, a thin sheet of polystyrene with cut out fragment shapes had been placed under the hardboard to act as separator).

The central section, then, awaits completion, while other areas of the Chi-Rho panel are also ready to be mounted. It is hoped that one day, at least this part of the Lullingstone restoration project will be completed, so that we can show what had actually decorated part of the Christian complex. This Antechamber wall-painting should awaken much interest. After all, the Lullingstone paintings are not only important for the study of Roman art but also for the study of early Christianity in Britain.

NOTES

1. G.W. Meates, *The Lullingstone Roman Villa* II (forthcoming).

2. G.W. Meates, *Lullingstone Roman Villa* 1955 fig. 13b.

3. G.W. Meates, *Lullingstone Roman Villa* 1955 fig. 12.

4. G.W. Meates, *The Lullingstone Roman Villa* II (forthcoming).

5. K. Painter, *The British Museum Quarterly* XXXIII (1969) Pl.67.

12. ROMAN WALL-PAINTING IN THE NETHERLANDS : A SURVEY

Eric M. Moormann

In the Netherlands, as in many other countries, wall-paintings dating from the period of the Roman occupation have been neglected for a long time. They did not seem to be important or numerous enough to make a reconstruction possible. In excavation reports plaster fragments were often not mentioned at all or only referred to in a brief note. Thus many finds were stored away in the cellars of museums and were never given proper attention in publications. The result is that they are difficult to locate, particularly because of the fact that the finds from one excavation are often divided among several museums or collections. The finds in the Roman villa at Stein, for example, were split up into four different collections.

J.E. Bogaers's work on the Gallo-Roman temples at Elst (Bogaers 1955), which has an exhaustive chapter on the paintings of these two sanctuaries, stimulated more intensive research. The result was that more attention was paid to wall decorations by subsequent excavators. Mention should be made of detailed articles on the paintings found at Nijmegen (Peters 1965-66, Peters 1969) and Rijswijk (Bloemers 1976, Bloemers 1978). Publications on finds at Druten, Aardenburg and some villas in Limburg are forthcoming (cf. Swinkels 1981). The finds from former excavations also received more attention from the archaeologists as a result of extensive research in other parts of the former Roman provinces. Thus it is possible to reconstruct and interpret the material found at one place by making use of parallels found in similar circumstances.

In this article a survey will be given of the wall-paintings known to us. On the basis of these data, although they presumably form only a small part of what must have existed in the way of paintings, we can get a reasonable idea of the mural decorations in the Roman Netherlands. The quality of the paintings rarely reaches the level of that in the Italian centres. The mural paintings in the countries surrounding Holland are often of higher quality than what has been found here. Only seldom do we come across valuable fragments as, for instance, at Voorburg, Elst, Bocholtz and Nijmegen.

Panels in combination with marbled dados were the most frequently applied types of mural decorations. At Elst, Druten and Nijmegen we could conclude this with the help of key-fragments, but also in cases where only a few fragments were found we can assume a similar type of mural decoration. In view of the generally poor quality it need not surprise us that panels are often completely white.

Candelabra that separate the panels from each other and thus enliven the wall are only known from Elst, Nijmegen and Voorburg. They can be related to the numerous candelabra in other parts of the northern provinces (Peters 1979 discusses this relation in greater detail).

Figurative representations can be found at Aardenburg, Voorburg and Nijmegen. In the latter place the rare occurrence of a representation of a garden draws our attention.

Marbling is present in many variations: not only simple splashing but also more intricate patterns were frequently applied. The imitation of *giallo antico*, especially the so-called Chemtou-marble, is applied most frequently; it was apparently very popular in the whole of the Roman empire (cf. Eristov 1979:696). Sometimes we find green or red porphyry. Most imitations are not based on existing types of marble. Imitations of real *crustae* do not occur frequently, except in the case of the elaborate socle of Aardenburg (cf. Abad Casal 1977-1978 for examples in Spain).

Wall-paper patterns are known from Nijmegen and Rijswijk. They constitute richer decorations. The lozenge-pattern of Bocholtz, even if this only formed a dado decoration, can be related to this type.

The often incomplete descriptions of buildings and finds in former publications make it very difficult to know the precise spot where plaster was found and consequently the room or rooms to which the decoration(s) belonged. It is therefore difficult to draw more general conclusions about the use of decorations in specific rooms or about the status of decorations and rooms. It can be assumed that the presence of paintings indicates a relatively rich building but we cannot arrive at a definitive conclusion.

With respect to the places of origin of the finds we can note that places along the Limes and villas in South-Limburg provide most of the known paintings. It is likely that also in other parts of Limburg and in North-Brabant villas might be found. The recent excavations at Hoogeloon near Eindhoven strongly point in that direction. Military and civilian settlements along the rivers Waal and Rhine could produce more material.

The paintings themselves do not provide many clues as to the dating. It was only at Elst and Nijmegen that mural decorations could be accurately dated, since other evidence was available.

In most cases paintings in the South-Limburg villas will have been applied in the second century A.D. These villas were often built as early as the end of the first or the beginning of the second century. They were deserted in the third century when tribes from outside the empire began to penetrate.

Decorations in other settlements will probably also have to be dated to the second century. The only exceptions are the paintings in Nijmegen and Elst, dated in the second half of the first century, and those from Rijswijk, painted in the first half of the third century.

Catalogue

The finds are arranged in groups according to the original

function of the buildings and sites. The first group is formed by temples, the second by civilian and military settlements and the third by villas. Within these groups the find-spots have been arranged in alphabetical order.

Preceding every place-name we find a number that corresponds with a number on the map (fig.12.1). Following the place-name the year(s) of research is (are) given in subsection a. Under b we find the present depository with reference number. The present depository of a number of finds is not known. There are fragments of unknown origin in the Rijksmuseum van Oudheden (Leyden) and the Bonnefantenmuseum (Maastricht). Under c publications are mentioned in which paintings are referred to.

One or more of these subsections are absent in cases where no data are available.

Finally there follows a short description of finds and reconstructions, if any, and if possible, reference will be made to the articles in question. Descriptions, which are often short, notably in excavation-reports, will be quoted in full since they are not easily accessible and quite often provide the only available information. Dutch texts will be given in English translation.

I Temples

1 a Elst 1947
   b Elst, Dutch Reformed Church
      Nijmegen, Rijksmuseum G.M. Kam, find no. 109
   c Bogaers 1955, 91-137

The paintings of the first temple can be dated between 50 and 65 A.D. It is impossible to arrive at a complete reconstruction of the decoration systems. Only three types of dado can be distinguished (Bogaers 1955, 124-125). The first two types consist of marbling with splashes on a white or yellow ground; in the third type the surface of the dado is mainly green.

Virtually complete systems could be reconstructed belonging to the second temple. The bases of the dados consist of coloured bands. Above we get panels with diagonally crossing lines, reaching a height of at least 72 cm. The panels are separated from each other by candelabra. J.E. Bogaers dates these frescoes to the beginning of the Flavian times.

It is not clear whether the outer walls were decorated or not (Bogaers 1955, 125-134).

2 a Rijsbergen 1842
   b 's-Hertogenbosch, Noordbrabants Museum, inv. no. D576-D581
   c Janssen and Cuypers 1844
      Hermans 1865, 71
      Bogaers 1955, 34-37

Some traces of a temple were found at Rijsbergen. An inscription with the name Sandraudiga indicates that there had been a sanctuary dedicated to this local goddess (Bogaers 1955, 34-37).

Some very small pieces of wall-painting were discovered and

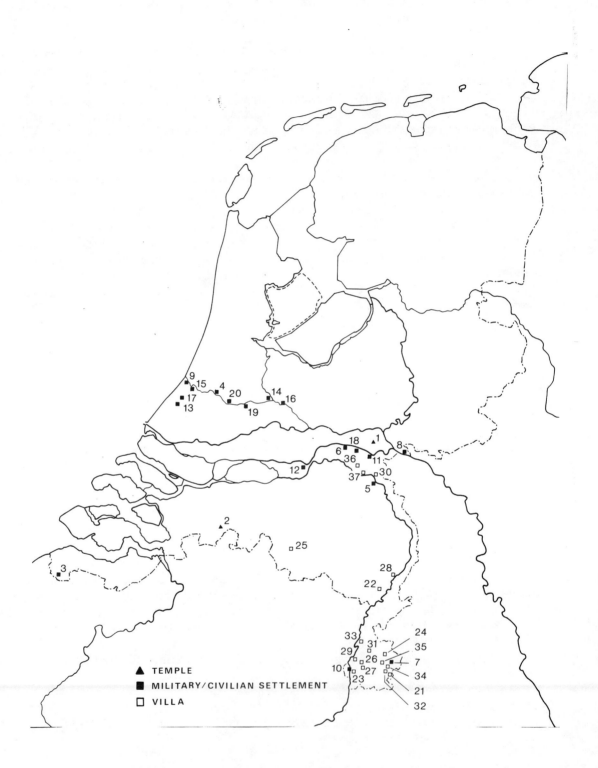

TEMPLE
MILITARY/CIVILIAN SETTLEMENT
VILLA

Fig.12.1: Findspots of Roman Wall-painting.

described by L.J.F. Janssen and P. Cuypers. 'Seven pieces of wall-plaster and masonry, of which four were painted in red, brown, dissolving in yellow, white with red stripes and green with brown stripes. The fragments have a fine mortar. One white fragment mainly consists of little pieces of broken tiles, and other pieces have a coarse mortar with fragments of shells and on their backs imprints of straw.' (Janssen and Cuypers 1844, 163).

C.R. Hermans writes: 'Some pieces were smooth on one side with yellow, brown and green stripes varying in width, sometimes turning into a lighter colour, which colours, however, exposed to the air, lost much of their clarity and lustre.' (Hermans 1865, 71).

An attempt at reconstruction was made by J.E. Bogaers but has not yet been published.

II Civilian and Military Settlements

3   a Aardenburg 1971
     b Aardenburg, Gemeentelijk Museum
       Middelburg, Zeeuws Museum

During the digging campaign of 1971 a large amount of some 1000 pieces of wall-plaster was found in a big pit near a large building (Trimpe-Burger 1971, 141-144, has a brief section on this excavation, but does not mention plaster). The fragments, mixed with clay and rubbish, had been used to construct a pavement. Research into these finds has so far resulted in the discovery of at least two decoration systems.

1) Panel decorations: the upper part displays green garlands with red dots and yellow creepers on a white ground; the panels are lined by means of frames consisting of red bands and black lines; the dado is decorated with a simple marbling, i.e. splashes on a white ground (fig.12.2).

2) Panel decoration, consisting of a dado richly decorated with a large porphyry tondo on a white ground with light brownish veining (cf. Eristov 1979, 696 for this type of marbling and Abad Casal 1977-1978 for other examples of such *crustae*) and an upper part which resembles the first system. Garlands are lacking. The beads in the four angles can be compared with those at Elst and Druten. (Fig.12.3).

Other fragments will have belonged to different systems. Numerous pieces showing marbling, e.g. green porphyry, the so-called *lapis lacedaemonius* (cf. porphyry tondo at Nijmegen: Peters 1965-1966, plate XIII A), and perhaps a tondo with floral and foliate patterns formed part of elaborate dados.

There are also indications for panels, consisting of a framework of leaves and creepers. A group of thin fragments with rough surfaces, finally, belonged to simple panel decorations as we know from Druten, or to a ceiling with imitation of cassettas.

4   a Alphen aan den Rijn 1978
     b Nijmegen, Katholieke Universiteit, Instituut Oude Geschiedenis
       en Archeologie, inv. no. AL 1978. 1. 1.

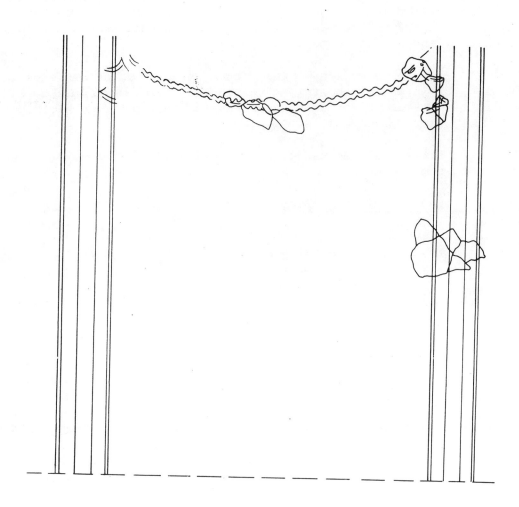

0   1m

Fig.12.2: Aardenburg (No.3) : Panel Decoration.

0   1m

Fig.12.3: Aardenburg (No.3) : Panel Decoration.

During a rescue excavation two fragments with a red surface were found.

5A a Cuijk (military settlement) 1937-1938, 1964, 1966
     b Nijmegen, Katholieke Universiteit, Instituut Oude
       Geschiedenis en Archeologie, inv. no. 1937. 21.
       1938. 139, 140, 238, 241, 261, 279
       Amersfoort, Rijksdienst voor het Oudheidkundig Bodemonderzoek,
       find no. 698, put 9 (box 160)
     c Willems 1937-1940
       Bogaers 1966 (no paintings mentioned)

Excavations by A.E. van Giffen in the 1930s and by J.E. Bogaers in the 1960s brought to light some pieces of wall-plaster. These were found not far from a temple, situated furthest to the west, in rubble that had been used to pave the temple floor. Willems writes that a 'large piece could be taken away.' (Willems 1937-1940, 45). Some display green leaves on a white ground.

5B a Cuijk (civilian settlement) 1977
     b Cuijk, private collection
     c Koeling and Koolen 1978

Non-professional archaeologists at Cuijk discovered the cellar of a Roman house in the actual centre of the village, outside the Roman castellum. Fragments of plaster are mentioned in their publication. 'The decoration of some pieces consisted of reddish-brown and greyish-silver bands on an ochre yellow ground. On the yellow surface of one fragment we can see a slender arched reddish-brown band and next to it traces of green.' (Koeling and Koolen 1978, 31).

6   a Druten 1974-1978
     b Amersfoort, Rijksdienst voor het Oudheidkundig Bodemonderzoek,
       inv. no. 1, 5, 9, 13, 14, 16, 17, 23-26, 28, 31, 33, 34, 39,
       40, 42, 44, 45, 46, 53-56, 59-61
       Wychen, Frans Bloemen Museum
     c Peters, Swinkels and Moormann 1978
       Swinkels 1981

Four nearly complete systems of panel decoration could be reconstructed. These belong to three buildings. The paintings can be dated to the second century A.D.

7   a Heerlen 1950
     b Heerlen, Thermenmuseum, inv. no. 95 and boxes 40, 93-101,
       134-148, 188-191
     c Bogaers 1950
       Maasgouw 1951
       Gielen 1966
       Jamar 1977

In a cellar of a house at Meezenbroek fragments were found in a rubbish pit in 1950. The pit formed part of a hypocaust. An attempt at reconstruction was made. 'It consisted of a reddish-brown panel, lined by a frame of green, yellow and greyish-black bands. The bands and the panel were divided by white stripes.' (Bogaers 1950, Maasgouw 1951, photograph in Jamar 1977, 15). These fragments prove that at least part of the paintings belonged to a dado (a plinth can clearly be distinguished).

Also in the Roman baths and in some neighbouring buildings fragments of paintings have been found. They do not provide enough information for a reconstruction.

In some rooms paintings were found in situ. All panels were red. In a room, labelled G, 'a fragment of a reveal of a door or window was found, painted with lines, arches and dots in black, white, yellow and red.' (Gielen 1966, 16 and 17, fig. 1). These reveal fragments resemble the similar pieces from Mook.

8 a Herwen en Aerdt
   b 's-Heerenberg, Huis Bergh
   c Bogaers and Rüger 1974, 90-92

In the polder, called Bijlandse Waard, one fragment of wall-painting was found. It must belong to the settlement which was the castellum Carvium, dating to the second century A.D. Some excavations carried out in this neighbourhood revealed traces of this military settlement.

9 a Katwijk aan Zee 1910-1911
   b Leyden, Rijksmuseum van Oudheden, inv. no. h. 1912/1. 69
   c Holwerda 1912
      Martin 1912

The excavation of a wooden building at Katwijk aan Zee did not provide sufficient information to determine the exact nature of the settlement. Only two fragments of plaster, displaying green plants on a white ground, were listed in the catalogue (Martin 1912, 62). They may belong to a dado like the one at Druten.

Ceramic finds proved that the building dated to the early Flavian period.

Later research has shown that the presumably civilian settlement Lugdunum is meant here, of which traces have been found at 'Klein Duin' and 'Zanderij Westerbaan'. This settlement is thought to have been inhabited from circa 50 to 250 A.D. (Bogaers and Rüger 1974, 36-39).

10 a Maastricht 1840
    c Leemans 1843, 38-61
       Habets 1881, 96-98

In 1840 some cellars were excavated in a house in Stokstraat, and a hypocaust was found. In room I traces of painting were found in situ. C.J.C. Leemans also discovered 'pieces of the plastered ceiling of the room' (Leemans 1843, 47), mentioned by Jos. Habets in his review of Roman habitation in Limburg: 'fragments de plafond peint' (Habets 1881, 98).

11A a Nijmegen (military settlement) 1962
     b Nijmegen, Rijksmuseum G.M. Kam, inv. no. 221, 339, 413, 900, 971-973, 1506, 1607, 1650-1651
        Amersfoort, Rijksdienst voor het Oudheidkundig Bodemonderzoek

        c   Peters 1965-1966
            Peters 1969
            Peters 1979

    Most fragments formed part of panel decorations. There are traces
of candelabra, painted between panels. Another panel decoration could
be reconstructed only partly.

    There is evidence for a garden view, a rather unique decoration
in the northern provinces.

    A reconstruction could also be made of what one could describe as
'flowered wall-paper'. A similar wall-paper decoration we know from
Rijswijk.

    The Nijmegen paintings can probably be dated to shortly after the
construction of the stone buildings by the Legio X Gemina between 85
and 90 A.D. They are of high quality and have smooth surfaces.

    Some additional finds, including fragments from the *canabae*, are
discussed by W.J.Th. Peters in a third article (Peters 1979).

11B   a   Nijmegen (Noviomagus)
      b   Nijmegen, Rijksmuseum G.M. Kam, inv. no. 7. 1968. 148
          Nijmegen, private collection
      c   Van Schevichaven 1904, 76-82
          Jamar and Thijssen 1968

    As early as the 17th century the historian Johannes Smetius
mentioned plaster which he has seen in situ: 'I have seen walls with
a smooth plaster surface, painted in perfectly fresh colours, while pots,
coins, tiles were dug up in my presence.' (cited by Van Schevichaven
1904, 79-80. According to him Smetius wrote it in *Antiquitates Neomag-
enses*, Nijmegen 1678, where this quotation, however, is not to be found.)

    The only evidence is provided by a small number of fragments.
These are occasional finds. It is not possible to reconstruct decoration systems on the basis of this material.

12   a   Rossum 1841
     c   Leemans 1842

    C.J.C. Leemans carried out a few minor excavations at Rossum, where
the Roman castellum Grinnes has to be located. Among other things he
saw 'a wall skilfully finished, painted in red and green colours on the
smooth side, which proves above all that the site must have been more
than a simple camp or watchtower.' (Leemans 1842, 129).

13   a   Rijswijk 1967-1969
     b   Amersfoort, Rijksdienst voor het Oudheidkundig Bodemonderzoek,
         find no. 19
     c   Bloemers 1976
         Bloemers 1978, II, 334-343

    In building 19. II. B a of a Cananefate settlement rich wall-
paintings were found. Two decoration systems could be reconstructed
by the excavator.

1) 'Wall-paper', consisting of a trelliswork with brown and yellow circles on a white ground which covers the complete wall.
2) Panel decoration, consisting of red and yellow panels outlined in black.

Perhaps there were also black panels for which, however, not enough evidence can be given.

The building as a whole can be dated to the time of the construction of the stone buildings around 230 A.D. It was one of the more luxurious constructions with a hypocaust. The excact function is unknown.

14 a Utrecht 1929-1935
   b Utrecht, Procinciaal Utrechts Genootschap
   c Van Giffen, Vollgraff and Van Hoorn 1934-1938

At least three buildings in the castellum Utrecht, according to the excavators the praetorium, a barracks for soldiers and a guard-house, were decorated with wall-paintings.

In the praetorium stucco was found in situ in section H 1, dating to the last period (IIb) of the castellum (Van Giffen, Vollgraff and Van Hoorn 1934-1938, IV, 143).

In the barracks the excavators found 'near all these walls pieces of plaster facing (approx. 3 cm thick), on the smooth side of which traces of red, green and yellow paint were still clearly visible.' (Van Giffen, Vollgraff and Van Hoorn 1934-1938, II, 40).

In the 'guard-house' fragments were found displaying 'a white ground on which thin red, green and yellow lines were painted, and foliate patterns similar to those from many Roman excavations. These fragments prove that the building was constructed in stone.' (Van Giffen, Vollgraff and Van Hoorn 1934-1938, III, 88). A timber construction, however, cannot be excluded. The building is dated to the last quarter of the second century.

15 a Valkenburg (Zuid-Holland) 1967
   b Leyden, Rijksmuseum van Oudheden, inv. no. h. 1933/12. 23, h. 1942, h. 1949/12. 4
      Amsterdam, Instituut voor Prae- en Protohistorie

Only by chance some fragments were found at a place called 'De Woerd' in 1933 and shortly after World War II, where afterwards extensive excavations were carried out.

During excavations in the Roman castellum in 1967 also many pieces were found.

16 a Vechten 1892-1894
   b Leyden, Rijksmuseum van Oudheden, inv. no. f. 1892/11. 14
      Utrecht, Provinciaal Utrechts Genootschap
      Oosterbeek, private collection
   c Muller 1895

During excavations in the Roman castellum at Vechten some pieces of wall-plaster were found: 'one with a red surface, one with yellow

lines on a white ground, one with yellow and green surfaces, divided
by a white line, one with marks of red figures, seven pieces with a
green surface.' (Muller 1895, 143-144).

17 a Voorburg 1827-1833, 1908-1915
    b Leyden, Rijksmuseum van Oudheden, inv. no. AR 63-64A, h. 1908/
       10.3, h. 1949/12. 1-2
    c Holwerda 1923

As early as the beginning of the nineteenth century C.J.C. Reuvens
carried out excavations at the estate of Arentsburg at Voorburg near
The Hague (Holwerda 1923, 4-8). He found remains of a large stone
building. He thought that there must have been a Roman military settlement, a conclusion supported by J.H. Holwerda some 90 years later, who
was of the opinion that it was a naval station (Holwerda 1923, 25-29).
J.E. Bogaers, however, pointed out that the place must be Forum Hadriani,
the capital of the Cananefate tribe (Bogaers 1972, 318-326).

Reuvens had watercolours made of the painting fragments he found
in building I, which are now at Leyden (Rijksmuseum van Oudheden).
Holwerda published two of them (Holwerda 1923, plate III fig. 5). There
must have been red panels framed by broad bands which were furnished
with grotesque candelabra on a black ground between fluted marble
columns. The bases of these candelabra were formed by a cantharos or
crater resembling the one we know, for example, from Xanten (Horn 1971,
69).

The fragment displaying a griffin belongs to the top of a panel
(Holwerda 1923, plate III fig. 5). There is also one piece depicting
a bird.

Fragments with red surfaces and green garlands and creepers formed
part of another panel system.

Pieces with yellow garlands on a white ground belong to a panel
decoration like the one found at Aardenburg (fig.2). The white plaster
still shows the curving guide-lines for the garlands.

During the excavations by Holwerda in the same building only a
few heavily damaged fragments of a dado were found. The bands must have
been arranged in the same way as at Elst in order to suggest a plinth.

18 a Winssen 1968
    b Nijmegen, Rijksmuseum G.M. Kam, inv. no. 4. 1969. 31
    c Bogaers 1968

During excavations near the 'Oude Veerhuis' remnants were discovered of a *statio benificiarii consularis* or a villa from the second
century A.D. Among the finds was a fragment of a dado with marbling:
yellow splashes on a pink ground.

19 a Woerden 1975-1977
    b Nijmegen, Katholieke Universiteit, Instituut Oude Geschiedenis
       en Archeologie, inv. no. 1975. 4. 1, 1975. 65. 1a, 1977. 120. 1.

From the Roman castellum Lauriacum only a few fragments with
red or white surfaces are mentioned.

20 a Zwammerdam 1968-1970
    b Amsterdam, Instituut voor Prae- en Protohistorie, inv. no. 20.
       242 z

Only a few fragments of wall-painting were found during extensive
excavations in the Roman castellum Nigrum Pullum. One 'fried egg' marbled
piece, found in a former bed of the river Rhine, should be noted.

III Villas

21 a Bocholtz (Vlengendaal) 1911, 1913
    b Maastricht, Bonnefantenmuseum, inv. no. Oud 370A
       Leyden, Rijksmuseum van Oudheden, inv. no. 1. 1914/12
    c Goossens 1918
       Liversidge 1969, 151-152

During excavations in the hamlet Vlengendaal a large villa dating
to the second and third century was unearthed. In room M a part of a
red dado was found: 'Reste von rotem Wandverputz befanden sich in der
Südecke noch am Ort und Stelle.' (Goossens 1918, 6). Unfortunately, no
photograph of the decoration was published.

In the hypocaust of room A a great number of plaster fragments
were found among earth and rubble. 'Die Farben, hauptsächlich rot und
grün, gelb und braun, sind besonders frisch erhalten geblieben. Versuche
eine Rekonstruktion der meistens lineären Figuren des Ornaments herzu-
stellen, hatten keinen Erfolg.' (Goossens 1918, 4).

A group of 31 pieces, not discussed by W. Goossens, clearly
belongs to one decorative system. On the basis of these fragments we
can reconstruct a decoration consisting of white, green and black
lozenges (fig. 12.4). These diamonds imitate blocks that jot out.
The green and black lozenges suggest shade. The size of the lozenges
and, therefore, of the panels cannot be calculated. Neither can we
reconstruct the direction of the lozenges, not even with the help of
brush marks. They probably only decorated a dado.

This pattern was called by Pliny the Elder *scutulatum (Naturalis
Historia* 36, 185) and is well-known from mosaics and paintings,
especially in the Casa dei Griffi in Rome, where panels in the main part
of the wall, dating to the early Second Style, show similar decorations.
Outside Rome at Agrigento (Sicily) a similar dado was found in the
Hellenistic-Roman quarter of the town. This decoration probably dates
from the first century B.C. Unfortunately these fragments are unpublished. They are on show in the Museo Archeologico at Agrigento. In
the northern provinces this Vlengendaal decoration is unique. No other
examples can be mentioned.

Some other fragments, among which are some well-preserved at
Leyden (Liversidge 1969, 151-152), belong to a dado with an imitation
of *giallo antico*, as at Aardenburg, Mook and Stein.

22 a Haelen (Melenborg) 1848-1849
    b Leyden, Rijksmuseum van Oudheden, inv. no. G.L. 394-395
    c Habets 1881, 227
       Goossens 1925

As early as 1848 and 1849 minor excavations at Melenborg brought to

Fig.12.4: Bocholtz (No.21) : Lozenge Pattern.

light a Roman villa. Pieces of mural decoration came into the possession of the notary Ch. Guillon at Roermond. His collection was donated to the museum at Leyden in 1900.

The fragments which are now at Leyden display green splashes on a red ground. They belong to a marbled dado.

Jos. Habets, however, gives a description of other paintings: 'Le crépi des murs avait été orné de lignes rouges, noires ou vertes, tirées parallèlement au cordon (...) Nous avons découvert des lignes coloriées, pareilles à celles-ci dans les villas de Meerssen, Rondenbosch, Billich, Steenland, Backerbosch (here resp. nos. 29, 27, 31 and 23) et autres de notre province.' (Habets 1881, 227).

A later survey did not yield results concerning paintings. W. Goossens only mentions the older finds (Goossens 1925).

23 a Heer (Backerbosch) 1882
    b Leyden, Rijksmuseum van Oudheden, inv. no. 1. 1932/12. 4(old:
       H.h. 26-39 and H.h. 236-245)

In 1882 Jos. Habets excavated the remains of a Roman villa at Backerbosch. The generally thin and small fragments of wall-plaster appear to be of good quality. Lines and colours, mostly black and white, have been well preserved. Some lines have little blocks and beaded corners.

A floral pattern and a decoration of white panels with black frames can be distinguished as well. A reconstruction could not yet be made, although further research may yield better results.

24 a Hoensbroek (Schuureyck) 1885
    c Habets 1887

Remains of Roman buildings, including a bath with hypocaust, were excavated at Schuureyck in 1885. In one room, by Jos. Habets called *hibernaculum*, plaster was found, 'coloured red and white with black, yellow and green stripes and paint-work resembling marble.' (Habets 1887, 321).

25 a Hoogeloon 1951, 1980
    b Amsterdam, Vrije Universiteit
    c Beex 1953

G. Beex mentions some finds at Hoogeloon near Eindhoven, among which were some pieces of plaster, which shows that there must have been a Roman villa. Large excavations were carried out during the summer of 1980. Many fragments of wall-painting were found in robber trenches and a well. Most fragments have white surfaces. They belong to panel decorations.

26 a Houthem (Ravensbosch) 1922-1923
    b Leyden, Rijksmuseum van Oudheden, inv. no. 1. 1932/12. 4
    c Remouchamps 1925

Only 15 fragments of wall-painting have been found at the Roman villa at Ravensbosch, built in the second century A.D. and equipped with a bath. In room 10 red plaster, belonging to the lower part of the socle, was found in situ. Also on the outside walls of room 6, room 9 and room 10 plaster could be seen. A.E. Remouchamps thought that the function of the plaster was to make the walls 'impermeable' (Remouchamps 1925, 55-57). No illustration was added, but the places are marked on the plan (Remouchamps 1925, fig. 41).

The 15 fragments do not enable us to produce a reconstruction. Mention should be made of one fragment with a green plant on a white ground, similar to pieces found, for example, at Druten. The other fragments show nothing but a red or white surface.

The backs of all fragments show clear imprints of straw or reed.

27   a   Houthem (Rondenbosch) 1864
     c   Habets 1868

Minor excavations were carried out in 1864 at Rondenbosch. 'Les murs et les parois des chambres paraissent avoir été enduits d'un crépi de différentes couleurs. Les fragments trouvés offraient un fond rouge ou blanc, avec des lignes jaunes, vertes ou blanches; c'était le genre de décoration ordinaire des villa's. Il a été observé au Herkenbergh (here no. 29) et ailleurs.' (Habets 1868, 353). One piece with foliate pattern is shown in watercolours (Habets 1868, plate IV fig. 53). It resembles the pieces of plants found elsewhere, e.g. at Druten.

28   a   Kessel (Hout) 1942
     b   Leyden, Rijksmuseum van Oudheden, inv. no. 1. 1911/4 and Box 412

The results of research at the Roman villa at Hout were, unfortunately, never published. There must have been a luxuriously equipped villa with hypocaust rooms (Verslag 1942, 8).

Painted fragments show either red stripes on a white ground or a red surface, probably belonging to panels.

The backs of the fragments have clear marks of straw.

29   a   Meerssen (Herkenbergh) 1865
     c   Habets 1871

In a villa at Herkenbergh a few fragments were found 'à fond jaune, ornés de lignes vertes, rouges ou noires (...) Un seul fragment de crépi du Herkenbergh semble fair exception à la règle générale; c'est un dessin de feuillage de couleur verte.' (Habets 1871, 393, plate X fig. 1)

According to Jos. Habets the latter resembles a fragment from Houthem (Rondenbosch)(here no. 26).

30   a   Mook (Plasmolen) 1933
     b   Leyden, Rijksmuseum van Oudheden, inv. no. 1. 1933/3. 34 Nijmegen, Rijksmuseum G.M. Kam, inv. no. B.A. VI 3 and 10. 1936. 66 (also old nos. from Leyden)
     c   Braat 1934, 4-13

The large luxurious estate, a so-called *villa urbana,* excavated at Plasmolen was situated on a hill ('Kloosterberg') and possessed porticos of 84 metres wide at both the front and the back. Not more than a few fragments of wall decoration were found. W.C. Braat assumes the existence of at least five systems of decoration, of which he describes three, one marbling and two groups of circles with flowers.

The first 'system' features as part of a dado decoration with marble imitation, consisting of the frequently used *giallo antico*, known from Aardenburg, Bocholtz and Stein.

Most of the fragments with flowers within half concentric circles and with blue balls have angles of 120 degrees and are therefore part of a reveal of a door or window. They resemble fragments of a reveal found at Heerlen. Unfortunately, it is not possible to reconstruct a complete system using these circles, but it is not unlikely that there was a 'wall-paper' decoration.

31 a Schimmert (Steenland and Billich)
    c Habets 1881, 227

Habets mentions in the description of the villa at Haelen (here no. 21) paintings found at Steenland and Billich, but in his reports concerning excavations at Schimmert (Habets 1878 and Habets 1882) no fragments of plaster were published or even mentioned. It seems, however, likely that these villas, dating to the second and third century A.D., possessed wall-paintings.

32 a Simpelveld 1933
    b Leyden, Rijksmuseum van Oudheden, inv. no. 1. 1941/1.1
    c Braat 1941

The masonry of the villa at Simpelveld was removed as early as the Middle Ages. 'The only architectonic fragments that can be mentioned are five pieces of painted stucco, belonging to a wall of a room. They display a very simple decoration, a surface of plain Pompeian red, framed by a white band, set off with a thin brown line against the red surface and further within the red plane we see a thin white line and a brown line at a distance of two centimeters of each other.' (Braat 1941, 46). These fragments belong to a panel decoration.

The villa can be dated to the end of the first or the beginning of the second century A.D., but it remained in use till the third century.

Later excavations in 1948 did not produce paintings.

33 a Stein 1925-1926
    b Leyden, Rijksmuseum van Oudheden, inv. no. 1. 1928/10. 74
       Maastricht, Bonnefantenmuseum, inv. no. 688
       Sittard, Streekmuseum 'Den Tempel'
       Stein, Archeologisch Reservaat, inv. no. VD 33-34
    c Holwerda 1928

In some of the rooms of the Roman villa at Stein large numbers of very small pieces of wall-painting were found. Reconstructions of three types of decoration were published by J.H. Holwerda, but he assumes the presence of some ten decoration systems. (Holwerda 1928, 35).

The 'fried egg' pieces, consisting of yellow dots on a green ground, formed part of a dado. Holwerda's reconstruction wrongly suggests a pattern that covers the complete wall.

Generally speaking one system was used in at least two other rooms, labelled 11 and 22. White panels were framed by two bands. In the panels circles and flowers were painted. Before paint was applied the decorations were sketched out in the wet plaster. Most panels have a striking feature. The upper angles are obtuse, as we know from some Pompeian paintings. In the northern provinces this is rather unique. The dado of this system consists of red, green or blue panels corresponding to the colours of the frameworks of the upper parts.

A third group of paintings from an unknown room resemble the system used in room 11 and room 22. The dado consists of a broad yellow band and a red oblong panel on top of that. The main part is formed by panels with brown or yellow frameworks on a white ground.

It is quite remarkable that no completely white fragments have survived. It could be that such pieces got lost during or shortly after the excavations.

A detailed publication of these fairly rich decorations is in preparation.

34 a Ubachsberg 1922
    c Remouchamps 1923

A.E. Remouchamps mentions plaster which he saw in situ in the Roman villa at Ubachsberg: 'plaster in which regular lines had been drawn in order to imitate a carefully constructed wall.' (Remouchamps 1923, 65). Unfortunately no illustration is available.

35 a Voerendaal 1892-1893, 1931, 1947-1950
    b Leyden, Rijksmuseum van Oudheden, inv. no. 1. 1953/2. 20
    c Braat 1953

At Voerendaal, not far from Heerlen, remains of a large estate were unearthed in 1892 and shortly after World War II. Part of the villa had been in use as a farm and there were also rooms for the owner and his family. In the bath section at the south-side, adjoining the private apartments, some fragments of wall-painting were found, displaying green and red surfaces (Braat 1953, 57).

'At the north side of room 18 remains were found of a fresco-painting, showing brown rosettes on a white ground, set in double red circles. Also fragments of what seem to be edges, in grey-blue, purple-red and green.' (Braat 1953, 58 and 72).

The villa must have been constructed in the early second century A.D. As early as the thirties of the third century the villa was abandoned during raids of invading Germans. Clear traces of fire suggest complete destruction of the building at this or a later period. There are no traces of further Roman occupation (Braat 1953, 75-76).

36 a Wychen (Tienakker) 1971
    b Wychen, Frans Bloemen Museum

c   Janssen 1971

Some fragments of wall-plaster were found in the Roman villa at Tienakker, among which 'pieces with flowers and foliate patterns in yellow, green, brown and red on a white ground.' (Janssen 1971, 14).

ADDENDUM

37   a   Heumen (Scheiwal, Overasselt) 1930
     b   Leyden, Rijksmuseum van Oudheden, inv. no. e. 1930/4. 2
         Wychen, Frans Bloemen Museum
     c   Braat 1934, 13-18

The fragments from the Roman villa at Overasselt, not far from Wychen, seem to belong to a decoration of white panels with red and green bands. W.C. Braat does not discuss the fragments which are now at Leyden.

ACKNOWLEDGEMENTS

A considerable part of this study would not have been possible without the help of Dr. P.Stuart (Leyden), Mrs. Drs. M.E.Th. de Grooth (Maastricht), A. Roebroek (Sittard), Rev. A.J. Munsters M.S.C. (Stein), J. Gielen (Heerlen), Ir. J.Trimpe Burger (Aardenburg), who gave me information about the collections of their museums.

I am also much indebted to Prof. Dr. J.E.Bogaers and Dr.J.K. Haalebos who provided valuable information about references and excavations, to Mrs. Ilja ten Brink and E.Ponten for the reconstructions and the map.

The text of this article was kindly translated by Drs. F.J.M. Blom. Finally I am most particularly grateful to Prof. Dr. W.J.Th.Peters and Drs. L.J.F. Swinkels with whom I spent many pleasant hours, working on paintings.

BIBLIOGRAPHY

Abbreviations: *BROB* : Berichten van de Rijksdienst voor het Oudheid-
                          kundig Bodemonderzoek

                 Bulletin : Bulletin des commissions d'art et d'
                          archéologie

                 OML : Oudheidkundige Mededelingen   uit het Rijksmuseum
                          van Oudheden te Leiden

                 Nieuwsbulletin KNOB : Nieuwsbulletin van de Koninklijke
                          Nederlandse Oudheidkundige Bond

                 Publications : Publications de la Societé Historique
                          et Archéologique dans le Duché de Limbourg

Abad Casal 1977-1978. Abad Casal, L., 'Las imitaciones de *crustae* en la pintura mural romana en España', *Archivo Español de Arquéologia*, 50-51 (1977-1978), 189-208.

Beex 1953. Beex, G., 'Toevallige vondst te Hoogeloon', *Brabants Heem*, 5 (1953), 113-115.

Bloemers 1976. Bloemers, J.H.F., 'Wandmalereien aus der römischen Siedlung in Rijswijk (Z.H.)', in: *Festoen*, Bussum, 1976, 75-108.

Bloemers 1978. Bloemers, J.H.F., *Rijswijk (Z.H.), 'De Bult', Eine Siedlung der Cananefaten*, 3 vols, Nederlandse Oudheden, 8, 's-Gravenhage, 1978.

Bogaers 1950. Bogaers, J.E., *BROB*, 1 (1950), aflevering 5, 9.

Bogaers 1955. Bogaers, J.E., *De Gallo-Romeinse tempels te Elst in de Over-Betuwe*, Nederlandse Oudheden, 1, 's-Gravenhage, 1955.

Bogaers 1966. Bogaers, J.E., 'Opgravingen te Cuijk', *Nieuwsbulletin KNOB*, 1966, 7e aflevering, ^{X}65-^{X}72.

Bogaers 1968. Bogaers, J.E., *Nieuwsbulletin KNOB*, 1968, 10e aflevering, ^{X}117.

Bogaers 1972. Bogaers, J.E., 'Civitates und Civitas-Hauptorte in der nördlichen Germania Inferior', *Bonner Jahrbücher*, 172 (1972), 310-333.

Bogaers and Rüger 1974. Bogaers, J.E. and Rüger, C.B., *Der Niedergermanische Limes*, Kunst und Altertum am Rhein, 50, Köln, 1974.

Braat 1934. Braat, W.C., 'Nieuwe opgravingen van Romeinsche villae', *OML*, Nieuwe Reeks, 15 (1934), 4-38.

Braat 1941. Braat, W.C., 'Nieuwe opgravingen van Romeinsche villa's in Limburg', *OML*, Nieuwe Reeks, 22 (1941), 39-51.

Braat 1953. Braat, W.C., 'De grote Romeinse villa van Voerendaal', *OML*, Nieuwe Reeks, 34 (1951), 48-79.

Byvanck 1947. Byvanck, A.W., *Excerpta Romana*, III, Rijks Geschiedkundige Publicatiën, 89, 's-Gravenhage, 1947.

Eristov 1979. Eristov, H., 'Corpus des faux-marbres peints à Pompéi', *Mélanges de l'Ecole francaise de Rome, Antiquité*, 91 (1979), 693-771.

Gielen 1966. Gielen, J., *Het land van Herle*, 16, no. 1 (1966), 16-17.

Goossens 1918. Goossens, W., 'Die römische Villa bei Vlengendaal', *Internationales Archiv für Ethnographie*, 24 (1918), 1-22.

Goossens 1925. Goossens, W., 'Onderzoekingen te Melenborg in de gemeente Haelen (L.)', *OML*, Nieuwe Reeks, 1 (1925), XXVII-XXXIII.

Habets 1868. Habets, Jos., 'Exploration d'une villa belgo-romaine au Rondenbosch à Houthem-Saint-Gerlach', *Publications*, 5 (1868), 347-393.

Habets 1871. Habets, Jos., 'Exploration d'une villa belgo-romaine au Herkenbergh à Meerssen', *Publications*, 8 (1871), 379-428.

Habets 1878. Habets, Jos., 'Une colonie belgo-romaine au Ravensbosch près de Fauquemont (2me article)-Exploration de la villa de Billich', *Bulletin*, 17 (1878), 343-364.

Habets 1881. Habets, Jos., 'Découvertes d'antiquités dans le Duché de

Limbourg', *Publications,* 18 (1881), 3-300.

Habets 1882. Habets, Jos., 'Une colonie belgo-romaine au Ravensbosch (pres de Fauquemont)', *Bulletin,* 21 (1882), 123-160.

Habets 1887. Habets, Jos., 'Overblijfsels van Romeinsche gebouwen met bad- en verwarmingstoestel te Hoensbroek', *Verslagen en Mededeelingen van de Koninklijke Academie, Afd. Letterkunde,* 3e Reeks, 4 (1887), 315-331.

Hermans 1865. Hermans, C.R., *Noordbrabant's Oudheden,* 's-Hertogenbosch, 1865.

Holwerda 1912. Holwerda, J.H., 'Opgravingen in het Klein-Duin te Katwijk Binnen', *OML,* 6 (1912), 48-53.

Holwerda 1923. Holwerda, J.H., *Arentsburg, een Romeinsch militair vlootstation bij Voorburg,* Leiden, 1923.

Holwerda 1928. Holwerda, J.H., 'Nederzettingen bij Stein aan de Maas', *OML,* Nieuwe Reeks, 9 (1928), 3-50.

Horn 1971. Horn, H.G., 'Wandmalereien aus Kanten', *Rheinisches Landesmuseum Bonn,* 2 (1971), 19-22.

Jamar 1977. Jamar, J.T.J., *Coriovallum. Kaleidoscoop van Heerlen in de Romeinse tijd,* Heerlen, 1977 (published in 4 languages).

Jamar and Thijssen 1968. Jamar, J.T.J. and Thijssen, J.R.A.M., *Nieuwsbulletin KNOB,* 1968, 8e aflevering, [X]84-[X]85.

Janssen 1971. Janssen, A.J., 'Romeinse villa op de Tienakker te Wychen', *Jaarverslag van de Archeologische Werkgemeenschap Nederland, Afd. Nijmegen e. o.,* 14 (1971), 13-14.

Janssen and Cuypers 1844. Janssen, L.J.F. and Cuypers, P., 'Oudheidkundige ontdekkingen aangaande den tempel der Dea Sandraudiga te Zundert in Noord-Braband', *Bijdragen tot den Vaderlandschen Geschiedenis,* 4 (1844), 160-163.

Koeling and Koolen 1978. Koeling, J. and Koolen, M., 'Een Romeinse kelder te Cuyk aan de Maas', *Westerheem,* 27 (1978), no. 1, 20-48.

Leemans 1842. Leemans, C.J.C., *Romeinsche Oudheden te Rossem in den Zalt-Boemelerwaard,* Leiden, 1842.

Leemans 1843. Leemans, C.J.C., *Romeinsche Oudheden te Maastricht,* Leiden, 1843.

Liversidge 1969. Liversidge, J., 'Furniture and Interior Decoration', in: Rivet, A.L.F., *The Roman Villa in Britain,* London, 1969, 127-172.

Maasgouw 1951. (Anonymous), 'Archaeologisch Nieuws', *De Maasgouw,* 70 (1951), 14-16.

Martin 1912. Martin, H., 'Overzicht der romeinsche vondsten bij de opgravingen te Katwijk in 1910 en 1911', *OML,* 6 (1912), 54-62.

Muller 1895. Muller, S., 'Verslag over de opgravingen van Romeinsche Oudheden te Vechten, gedaan (...) in de jaren 1892-1894', *Jaarverslag van het Provinciaal Utrechtsch Genootschap,* 1895, 122-169.

Peters 1965-1966. Peters, W.J.Th., 'Mural Painting Fragments Found in the Roman Castra at Nijmegen', *BROB,* 15-16 (1965-1966), 113-114.

Peters 1969. Peters, W.J.Th., 'Mural Painting Fragments Found in the Roman Legionary Fortress at Nijmegen, II', *BROB,* 19 (1969), 53-71.

Peters 1979. Peters, W.J.Th., 'Mural Painting Fragments Found in the Legionary Fortress and the Canabae Legionis at Nijmegen', *BROB*, 29 (1979), forthcoming.

Peters, Swinkels and Moormann 1978. Peters, W.J.Th., Swinkels, L.J.F. and Moormann, E.M., 'Die Wandmalereien der römischen Villa von Druten und die Frage der Felderdekoration in den europäischen römischen Provinzen', *BROB*, 28 (1978), 153-197.

Remouchamps 1923. Remouchamps, A.E., 'Opgravingen van een Romeinsche villa te Ubachsberg', *OML*, Nieuwe Reeks, 4 (1923), 64-77.

Remouchamps 1925. Remouchamps, A.E., 'Opgravingen van een Romeinsche villa in het Ravensbosch (L.), *OML*, Nieuwe Reeks, 6 (1925), 41-79.

Swinkels 1981. Swinkels, L.J.F., 'Mural Paintings from a Roman Villa at Druten, the Netherlands', *British Archaeological Reports*

Trimpe Burger 1973. Trimpe Burger, J.A., 'The Islands of Zeeland and South Holland in Roman Times', *BROB*, 23 (1973), 135-148.

Van Giffen, Vollgraff and Van Hoorn 1934-1938. Van Giffen, A.E., Vollgraff, C.W. and Van Hoorn, G., *Opgravingen op het Domplein te Utrecht*, 4 vols, Haarlem, 1934-1938.

Van Kouwen 1968. Van Kouwen, C.P.J., 'Wat bouwde de Romeinen 1700 jaar geleden in Winssen?', *Kontaktblad van de Historische Vereniging voor het Land van Maas en Waal en het Rijk van Nijmegen*, 6, august (1968), 12-14.

Van Schevichaven 1904. Van Schevichaven, H.D.J., *Penschetsen uit Nijmegens verleden*, III, Nijmegen, 1904.

Verslag 1942. (Anonymous), *Verslag van den directeur over het jaar 1942*, Leiden, 1942.

Willems 1937-1940. Willems, J., 'Opgravingen te Cuijk 1938', *Handelingen van het Provinciaal Genootschap van Kunsten en Wetenschappen in Noord-Brabant*, 1937-1940, 44-46.

13. MURAL PAINTINGS FROM A ROMAN VILLA
AT DRUTEN, THE NETHERLANDS

Louis J.F. Swinkels

From 1974 up to 1979 the State Service for Archaeological
Investigations in the Netherlands carried out excavations in the village
of Druten near Nijmegen that brought to light the remains of a large
villa estate of Roman date (Hulst 1978; 1980). During the excavations
a great number of wall-plaster fragments were discovered.

In this paper I will first describe the nature and size of the
estate and then give an account of the results of the investigation of
the wall-painting fragments (for a full account, see: Peters, Swinkels,
Moormann 1978).

1. The Estate

Druten is situated 12 miles west of Nijmegen on the south bank
of the river Waal (page 170, fig. 12.1, No.6). In an area measuring 150
by 145 metres approximately, remains were discovered of more than 20
buildings arranged according to a clear pattern (Fig. 13.2). An oblong
open area of about 115 by 70 metres forms the centre of the estate. Most
of the buildings are parallel to this central area orientated in an
eastern/western direction. In fact only one building was found to
deviate from this orientation. It is situated on the west side of the
central area. Apparently this is the main building, dominating the
entire estate by virtue of its position. It was timber built and a
portico surrounded it on three sides. Within the building one room was
constructed of stone. A wall built against it may have formed part of
a staircase hall leading up to a room on the first floor. A vault near
the stone room contained a large number of fragments representing two
different types of decoration.

Close to the main building and north of the central area a stone
building was found which the excavator interpreted as a bath. Inside
a big well at the back of this building over 200 wall-painting fragments had been dumped representing one single decoration system.

About one fourth of the total number of fragments in Druten were
discovered near three buildings situated in the south-west corner of
the central area. All three of them were made of wood and probably
served for inhabitation. The wall-painting fragments represent at least
two different decoration systems.

The buildings of the eastern area would mainly have served agricultural purposes and may be identified as stables, sheds, workshops,
and storage accommodation. The estate's division into a western area
for inhabitation and an eastern part for agricultural activities and
the dwellings of the farm-hands is well reflected in the wall-painting
finds. Measured in square metres almost 90% of the fragments belong to
the western part of the estate.

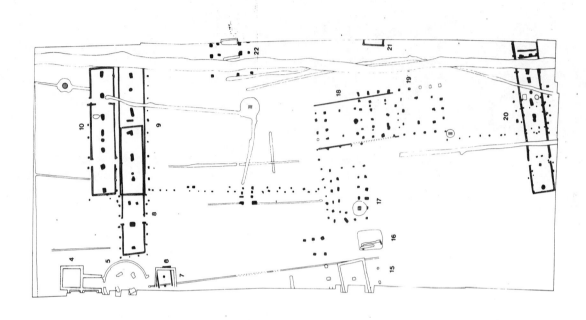

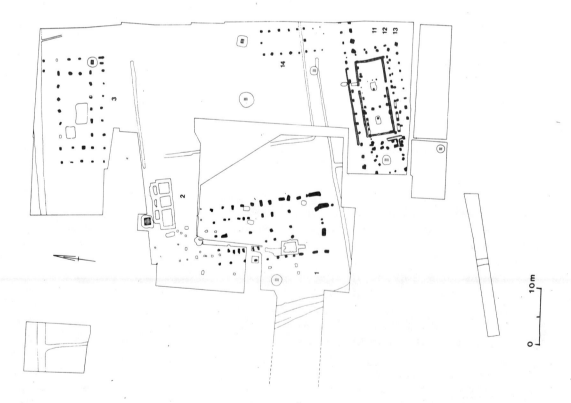

Fig.13.1: Druten, plan of the excavations.

The estate was built between 70 and 80 A.D. and originally merely consisted of the main building, building 11 south-east of it, and the two-nave buildings 8, 9, 10 and 20 in the east. Early in the second century the villa was extended with a number of new buildings, like the bath. Building 11 was supplanted by building 12, which was decorated with wall-paintings. Late in the second century A.D. the villa fell into decay. Inhabitation however lasted for some time into the third century.

The origin of the estate might be associated with the encampment of the Legio X Gemina in Nijmegen in the year 71 A.D. Simultaneously an extensive civil settlement, Ulpia Noviomagus, developed not far away from the legionary fortress. The Druten estate probably provided delivery of agricultural produce to the Nijmegen market.

2. The Fragments

Druten did not present any paintings in situ. All fragments were found in wells, rubbish-pits, and robber-trenches, apparently dumped there after the buildings had been pulled down.

About 2050 fragments in all were gathered from the estate measuring a total of almost 11 square metres. They can be related to at least 5 buildings. These figures indicate that only a minor part of the original wall-paintings has been preserved.

Consequently, it was not possible to reconstruct paintings by fitting fragments together. We did however manage in many cases to designate the fragments - on the basis of design - to a particular place on the wall, i.e. to the dado or to the main zone.

The fragments all belong to various representations of the panel system with the dado exhibiting imitation marbling and the main zone being divided into panels by means of straight lines. We were able to almost completely reconstruct 4 variants, which we labelled decorations A, B, C and D. Apart from location and design, composition of the mortar layers and imprints on the back of the bottom mortar layer provided evidence for reconstruction.

3. Reconstruction

The fragments discovered near the stone room in the main building represent two different decorations. This confirms the excavator's surmise that there must have been an upper storey to this room. One of the two decorations could be assigned to the ground floor on the basis of thicker mortar layers and damp traces in the dado fragments.

Decoration A (Fig. 13.2)

The ground floor decoration was by far the richest of the entire estate. On the dado marble was imitated by splashing red and black spots onto a yellow ground. The main zone consists of red panels framed in bands of yellow and black.

Reconstruction is based on four key fragments only. All the other fragments, though, confirm the picture emerging from those four. Three adjoining fragments show a panel corner and at the same time reveal how the main zone was marked off from the dado. Round the red panel runs a

0　　　　　　　　　　　　　　　　　1m

Fig.13.2:   Druten, Decoration A.

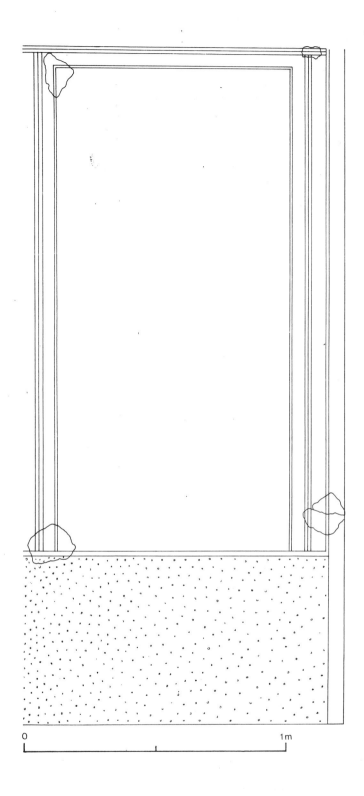

0　　　　　　　　　　　　　　　1m

Fig.13.3: Druten, Decoration B.

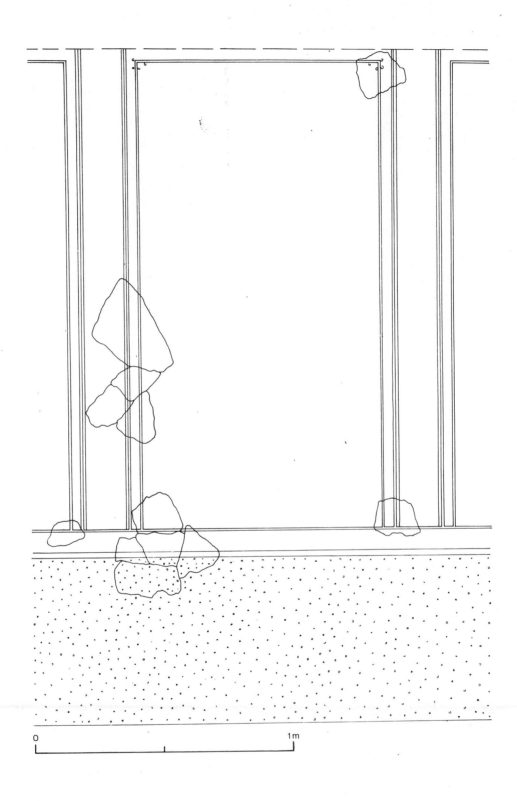

Fig.13.4: Druten, Decoration C.

yellow band, round that a black band. Moreover, these three fragments
prove that the decoration was enclosed by a vertical green band in the
corners of the room.

It remains uncertain what was in between the panels. Probably
they were separated by means of black division strips. Nor is it known
in what way the decoration was marked off at the top.

The stone room measured 3.70 metres by 2.10 metres inside. Consequently the long walls had space for 3 panels each of 1 to 1.10 metres,
depending on how broad the strips were. The short walls could take
only 2 panels which must have been somewhat broader than those on the
long walls.

Decoration B (Fig. 13.3)

The fragments of the second decoration, ascribed to the first
floor apartment above the stone room, make up about one third of the
total number of fragments discovered at Druten. The decoration consists of a pink dado splashed with black, yellow, and red spots, and
a white main zone divided into panels by means of narrow lines. On the
inside of each panel runs a single yellow line, on the outside a
double black-beige line.

Reconstruction was based on 5 key fragments. One of these shows
the pink dado marked off from the main zone by a red band. Two other
fragments reveal the upper demarcation of the panels. The double black-
beige line probably ran right across the wall. A vertical yellow band
enclosed the decoration in the corners of the room. Just as on the
ground floor the panels were over one metre broad.

Decoration C (Fig. 13.4)

In a well near the bath north of the main building was a second
group of fragments, all representing a single decoration system. It is
very similar to our Decoration B, though somewhat richer and more
neatly finished.

In this decoration too, marble was imitated on the dado by
splashing black, white, and grey spots onto a pink ground. The white
main zone was divided into panels marked off by black lines on the
inside and a double black-red line on the outside.

Again, reconstruction was based on a small number of key fragments. Five adjoining pieces show a pink dado separated from the main
zone by a black line and a red band. The panel forms may be deduced from
several fragments. The distance between the two demarcation lines varies
among the fragments, so that we may assume that the panels were not all
of the same size.

At the top, the black demarcation line was decorated with tiny
black beads at the corners of the panels. We assume that the panels
were enclosed at the top by a double black-red line running right
across the wall, just as in Decoration B, but we found no fragments
to substantiate this assumption.

Of the 221 fragments from the well, 3 could in no way be fitted

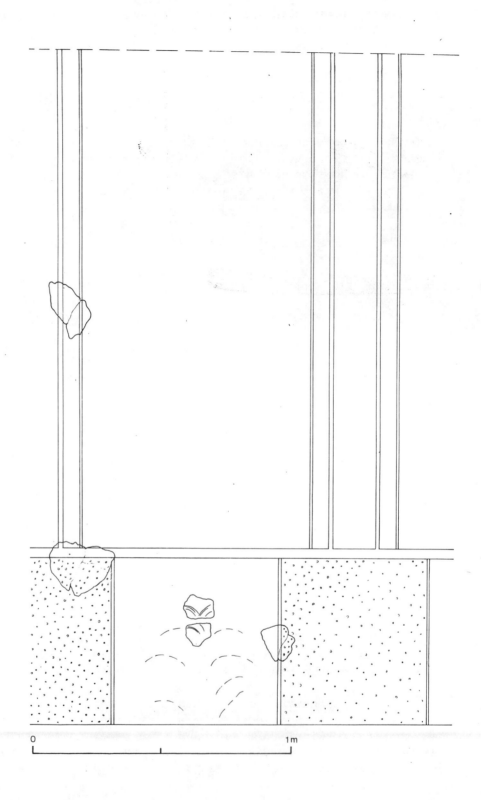

Fig.13.5: Druten, Decoration D.

into the reconstruction. Possibly they belonged to an upper zone, but it is unknown how this zone was decorated and in what way it was linked to the main zone.

The walls of the biggest room in the bath were approximately four and a half metres long. Thus there was room for either three panels measuring 1.30 to 1.35 metres, or four panels of about one metre. Four panels would probably imply a central panel and two half panels in the corners.

Decoration D (Fig. 13.5)

In another well near building 12, south-east of the main building, a third group of fragments were discovered representing one single decoration system. In this system the dado is subdivided into splashed and unsplashed white areas. Foliate motifs decorate the unsplashed parts. The main zone is plainly divided into panels defined by a framework of two lines.

The amount of key fragments for reconstructing Decoration D is again small. It could not be proved that the foliate motifs really belonged to the dado, that is, not purely on the evidence of the fragments. Nevertheless, this solution seems most likely if we consider similar examples of dado decoration throughout the Roman provinces.

A red band marks off the dado from the main zone. The panels are enclosed by a black line and a red band. The upper limits of the main zone remain unknown.

Other Decorations

Any other panel decorations Druten may have had (and there were at least four decoration systems additional to the systems described in this paper) cannot be reconstructed, due to the inadequate number of fragments. It is clear though that all walls were decorated alike. Dados invariably consist of black, red, pink, or yellow grounds, in many cases splashed. The main zone is always white and divided into panels by straight lines in a number of different ways.

Dating

The paintings can only be dated on the basis of accompanying archaeological material. Decorations A and B are late first century A.D. or early second century. Decorations C and D are somewhat younger and date at least after the year 125. Probably all the additional fragments can also be assigned to the second century.

4. Summary

The Druten villa estate possessed wall decorations that were very modest in design if we compare them to other wall-paintings found in North West Europe. The panels' geometric rigidity is never interrupted by garlands or candelabra. None of the fragments show any trace of a figure-scene. Only Decoration D is enlivened by floral designs in the dado and even these do not escape a rather dull schematization.

Yet I should like to conclude by stressing the relative importance of such modest panel decorations as in the Druten finds. There is no doubt the paintings added considerably to the status of both villa and occupants, especially when we consider the rather modest appearance of the buildings. Therefore I think that, if only from a sociological point of view, the simplest of panel decorations deserve our full attention.

ACKNOWLEDGEMENT

I should like to thank Mr. Hans Heijhuurs for translating the Dutch text into English.

BIBLIOGRAPHY

Hulst, R.S., 1978. 'Druten-Klepperheide, Vorbericht der Ausgrabungen einer römischen Villa', *BROB,* 28, 133-151.

Hulst, R.S., 1980. 'Een Romeinse villa bij Druten', *Hermeneus,* 52, No.2, 117-127.

Peters, W.J.Th., Swinkels, L.J.F., & Moormann, E.M., 1978. 'Die Wandmalereien der römischen Villa von Druten und die Frage der Felderdekoration in den europäischen römischen Provinzen', *BROB,* 28, 153-197.

Abbreviation: *BROB* : Berichten van de Rijksdienst voor het Oudheidkundig Bodemonderzoek

14. SOME MOSAICS AND MURALS IN ROMAN TRIPOLITANIA

David E. Johnston

When we consider the pictorial arts of Roman North Africa, it is the superb mosaics that come most readily to mind. Indeed, Africa has been quoted in discussion as an area where there was no tradition of mural art and where painters were unobtainable; mosaic remained the dominant art form - by default, as it were. I have since had the privilege of being allowed to study some of the wall-paintings and mosaics in the museums of Roman Tripolitania through the kindness of the Department of Antiquities of the Socialist People's Libyan Arab Jamahiriya; and I was deeply impressed by the quantity and quality of the wall-paintings.

This note, therefore, seeks to redress the balance and to draw attention to the importance of this material in the artistic development of North Africa. It makes no claim to original scholarship, as this has been provided over the last 55 years or so for both media by several scholars, notably A. Aurigemma (1926, 1960, 1962), A. Di Vita (1964, 1966 and an unpublished lecture to the Society for Libyan Studies in 1978), W. Dorigo (1971), K.M.D. Dunbabin (1978) and many others. What follows is a record of personal observations that is naturally influenced by the work of those who have made these mosaics and murals their special study.

Aurigemma first drew attention to the intimate link between the designs on murals and mosaics in the villa at Dar Buc Ammera, Zliten. It should be emphasised, however, that the mosaics are manifestly of widely differing dates, and that his dating has been the subject of considerable dispute.[1] In fact, there is very little stratigraphic evidence for dating works in either medium, and arguments for constructing a chronological series rest on purely stylistic comparisons, some of which are ingenious and occasionally far-fetched. This is not the place to reopen this difficult debate.

With the exception of Aurigemma's basic (and seldom quoted) publications of the earlier discoveries, the murals have not been well served in illustration by their partial republication in specialist works. On inspection, however, two things are perfectly clear: first, that - in spite of the fragmentary nature of the material - the close relationship of mosaic and mural decoration was characteristic of all Tripolitania, at all periods. And further, that we are justified in treating both as two aspects of the same art form - not only in treatment, but also in the subject-matter which forms a substantial common ground. Second, that Tripolitania was the meeting-ground of artists and artistic influences from an interesting diversity of sources - Punic, Hellenistic, Alexandrian and Roman - at different times. It is these strands that form the substance of this note.

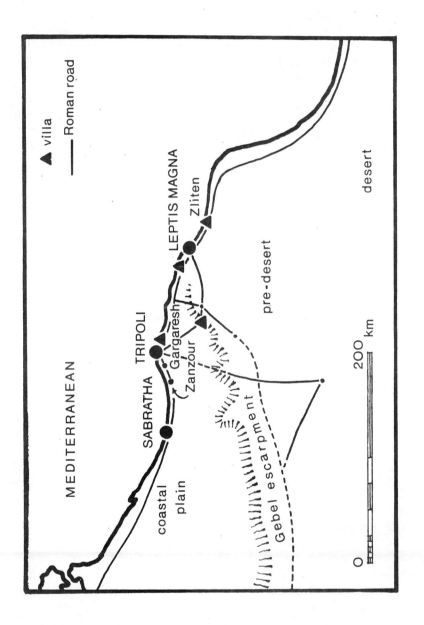

Fig.14.1: Map showing sites mentioned in the text.

Our selection starts with the little known (and apparently unpublished) tomb at Zanzour, some 6 km to the west of Tripoli on the road to Sabratha. Discovered in 1959, it is preserved beneath a small museum containing evidence for Punic and Roman settlement and a cemetery nearby. The tomb is dated from its contents to the first half of the first century AD. Simple painted flowers and festoons on a white ground accompany two figured scenes depicting the journey of the soul across the Styx to Hades, and its subsequent return to a new life. Winged erotes hover above. The impressionistic style of the small, wraith-like figures would not be out of place in one of the catacombs of Rome; Di Vita, however, recognises a technique that is common at Alexandria. On the other hand, the cycle of death and rebirth has its roots in the Greek and Hellenistic world, from which it is borrowed. Moreover, Di Vita draws attention to the figure of the deceased (perhaps even a priest of the mysteries) who is shown burning incense - a Punic or Neo-Punic element. In Tripolitania, the more distant Punic settlements did not suffer the abrupt extinction in 146 BC suffered by those nearer to Carthage. Cultural continuity is evidenced by a consciously neo-Punic element in sculpture and architecture, notably in the ubiquitous obelisk-tombs, and in the bilingual inscriptions set up in the major cities until the end of the first century AD.

The Hellenistic 'borrowings' are our second strand. For example, the fine lion's head (undated) in the centre of the Triumph of Liber Pater mosaic in the House of Liber Pater at Sabratha[2] is a familiar motif that can be traced back to the pebble-mosaics of c.300 BC at Pella. The fine painting of Dionysus on the panther from Zliten is another stock figure;[3] (Pl.14.3) the precisely similar figure at Pella has been traced back conjecturally to a painting by Xeuxis, and other examples are numerous.

Alexandrian 'influence' and direct 'borrowings' in our region can usefully be distinguished. To the first is ascribed a layout that seems to be confined to mosaics. Emblemata are now framed, not by the usual lines of geometrical ornament, but by broad figurative strips; these last are sometimes composed of further small emblemata in series inviting the spectator to walk around the composition studying the details of the border. Alternatively, as in the mosaic of the Seasons from Zliten, these scenes are arranged in vertical strips at the sides, giving a vertical axis to the whole and a single viewpoint. Perhaps the ultimate in figured borders is that of the Amphitheatre Mosaic from Zliten, where the central area of opus sectile and xenia emblemata is utterly eclipsed by the exciting border scenes. On the other hand, Alexandrian 'borrowings' are quite clear in the subject-matter of both mosaics and paintings - an intense preoccupation for a century or so with Nilotic scenes that was, of course, not confined to the North African provinces. An outstanding illustration of this, in the style of full realism associated with Alexandrian Hellenism, is the mosaics from the House of the Nile at Leptis Magna.[4] Rostovtzeff has observed that the four main panels were probably inspired by poems or epigrams of Hellenistic or Roman date. One is an allegory of the fertility of the Nile. 12 cupids (instead of the usual 16) equal the number of cubits for the water-level as measured by the Nilometer shown on the right; two nymphs (Memphis and Anchirroe?) symbolise the Sudan. In this house distinct Alexandrian influence has been noted by Aurigemma in at least two other scenes - those of amorini in a harbour and of the adornment of Pegasus. Other Nilotic scenes abound in painting, such as the battle of the pygmies (in reed-boats) with the cranes, from Zliten[5] and in mosaic, such as the similar scene from the baths at Wadi-es-Zgaia (Fonduk-en-Nagazza). The painted Nilotic landscapes of the *piscina* of the Hunting Baths at Leptis Magna are among the less well known surprises in that remarkable building.[6]

Finally, the inspiration, if not the actual work, of orthodox Roman artists accounts for some of the most ambitious decorative mural schemes. Simple but colourful geometrical designs can now be seen, preserved *in situ* in one or two of the more recent excavations, such as Regio VI at Sabratha or the houses by the pottery works at Gargaresh. But it is in the museums that we can study the more dramatic examples. Appropriately, the House of the Tragic Actor at Sabratha had theatrical schemes that would be described as Style IV at Pompeii, though Aurigemma believed that this essentially Roman art reached Tripolitania not direct, (Pl.14.1) but probably via Alexandria.[7] To be sure, this example lacks the feeling of luminous space, the architectural depth and the concealed light-sources of the best Pompeian essays in this fine Baroque medium. The ensemble at Sabratha must have looked rather crowded and incoherent; but even in its fragmentary state its inventiveness is breathtaking. The true quality of its artists shows, here and at other comparable sites, in the details that have come down to us as tantalising fragments. The grotesque and realistic tragic masks must rank among the most powerful painting to be found anywhere in the Roman world.[8] A more gentle, but equally moving, female head is preserved from an unnamed house near the Byzantine walls at Sabratha.[9] In a more impressionistic vein, the scenes from everyday life that were set, as pictures, in panels - here and elsewhere - form an unrivalled pictorial archive. Most notable in this genre are the better known scenes from Zliten, but at Sabratha there is also such a fantasy view of a house by the sea.[10] (Pl.14.2). Part of the house is seen at the back of this fragment, towered and colonnaded, while a massive masonry pier, adorned with mouldings, a sculptured (?) panel and a statue at its seaward end, reaches towards the viewer to enclose one side of a small private harbour in which the inevitable men in boats can be made out.

The reality behind this fantasy can now be seen at Zliten itself, where the excavated remains of a remarkable *villa maritima* can be visited. Today, all traces of the harbour works has vanished, and only the top of a flight of steps remains to remind us of them. But the villa is the perfect illustration of the Roman love of structures that seemed to conquer the very sea; structures which - in Horace's memorable passage (*Od.3,1,29-3* - caused even the fish to feel the ocean contracting *iactis in altum molibus*. Like nearly all the known luxury villas of Tripolitania it is in the coastal strip, in this case on three main areas specially levelled from the rocky coast. The least well preserved buildings are the Bath Suite (C), whose confused and fragmentary structures contained some paint-ings of a later date than those of the main residential block. The Baths adjoin a central Court (B) whose principal feature today is an elongated surface of herringbone brick paving that conceals a long subterranean cistern with draw-holes at the ends. The main Residential Wing backs against the rocky hillside into which it is set. To seaward the ground is built up to form a level garden extending over a large vaulted cistern; this marked the edge of the garden, from which one can still look down at the waves lapping the very feet of the man-made structures seemingly built to defy them. The garden is separated by a path from a long colonnaded portico (later filled in by a solid wall with windows); four column-bases survive from what must have been a small loggia looking back towards the house, and the path accompanied two semicircular *ex hedrae*, one of which at least had a mosaic (now a fragment only, showing the tail of a peacock). In this way the interior décor was extended into the garden. (Fig.14.2).

Plate 14.1. Reconstruction of wall decoration, House of the
Tragic Actor, Sabratha.

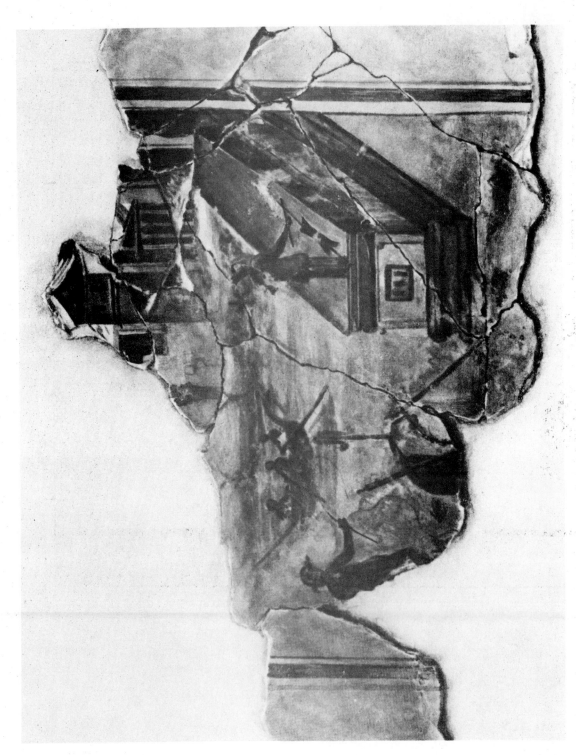

Plate 14.2. Sea view with houses. House of the Tragic Actor, Sabratha.

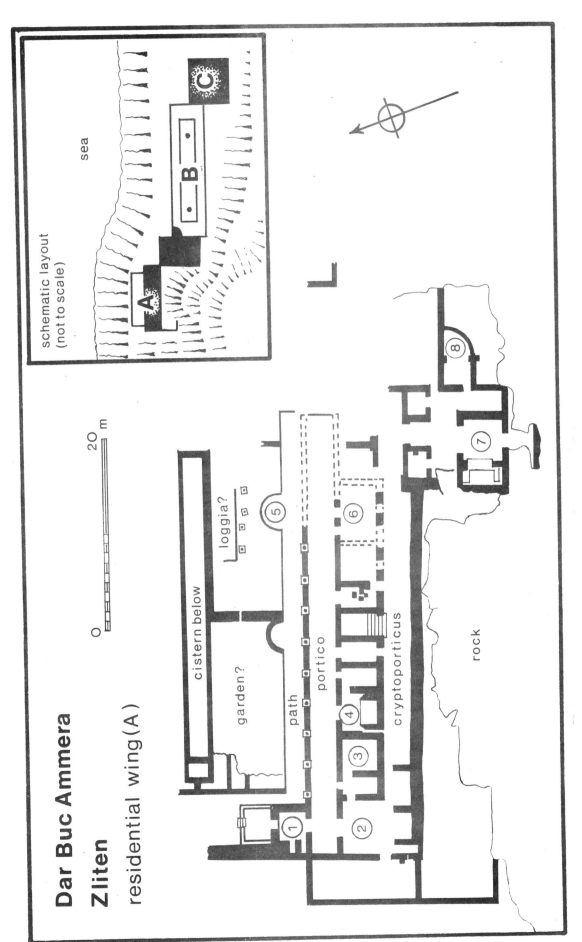

Fig.14.2: Plan of the villa at Dar Buc Ammera.

Dar Buc Ammera

Zliten

residential wing(A)

schematic layout
(not to scale)

sea

garden?

cistern below

loggia?

path

portico

cryptoporticus

rock

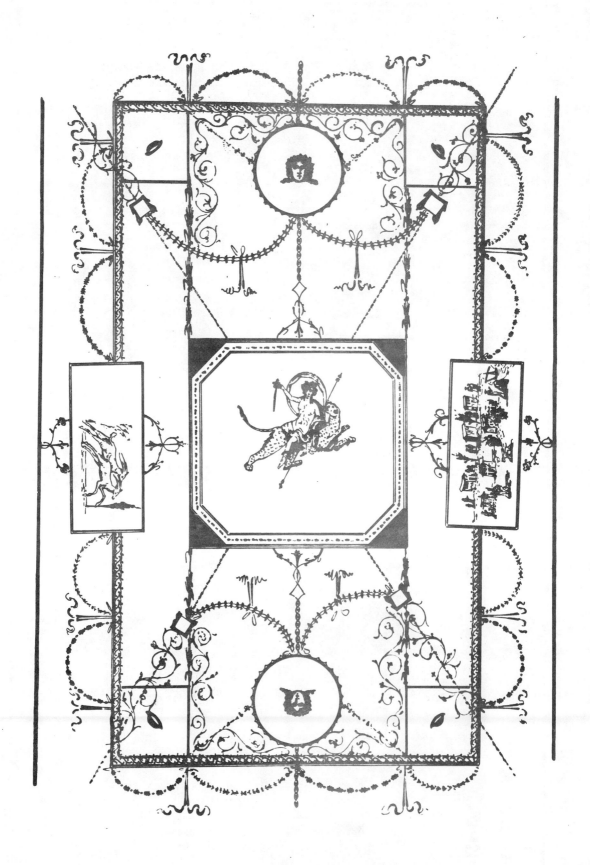

Plate 14.4. Detail of village from Plate 14.3.

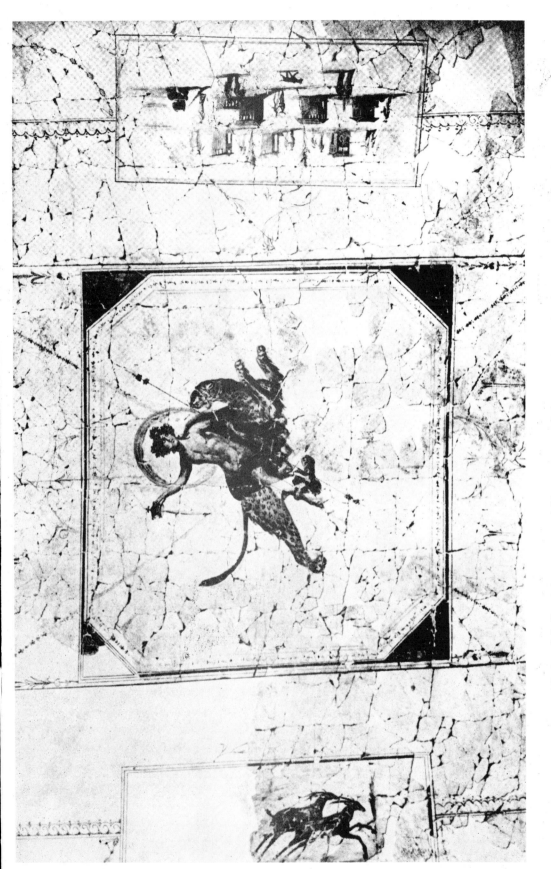

Plate 14.3. Dionysos riding a panther. Vault of Cryptoporticus, Dar Buc Ammera.

Fig. 14.3. Design from the vault of the Cryptoporticus, Dar Buc Ammera. F. Grosse.

The house itself was a long range of rooms, decorated with mosaics and doubtless with murals, with a simple wing enclosing the western flank of the garden. This, too, had its mosaic, an elaborate (but fragmentary) circular design. The portico was tessellated throughout its length, with a simple geometrical scheme, preserved in situ. The largest room, at the western end, contained the most famous mosaic,[2] showing scenes in the amphitheatre.[11] These form a continuous strip around a floor of mixed media, opus sectile and mosaic emblemata with fish.[12] The mixture of media is one striking feature of the decorative whole on this site, comprising opus vermiculatum, mosaic tessellation, opus sectile, wall-painting and stucco. Mosaic no.3 is of mixed styles and dates, comprising tile-mounted emblemata of the Seasons with panels showing coarsely depicted nilotic scenes, the whole in a setting of opus sectile in precious coloured marbles. Opus sectile recurs in the next room (4) with black-and-white lozenges, while the end room (6) once had an elaborate composition of geometrical panels in mosaic. A curious group of private rooms at the south-east corner, slightly set back, contained an important series of rural and nilotic scenes, some of which are still in situ, and the most withdrawn room of all (8) was decorated by a truly amazing mosaic in opus vermiculatum of a peopled scroll – 'The mosaic of the Acanthus Volutes' as it is often known[13] – and wall decorations to match.

The long range of rooms evidently had an upper storey, again with mosaics, to judge from the fragmentary emblemata found in the excavations. This upper floor, connected by stairs, extended over a long, vaulted cryptoporticus or corridor, whose rear wall was set against the quarried rock. The plastered vault had collapsed and was skilfully excavated and restored by the Italian excavators, providing evidence for a virtually complete decorative scheme and some fine painted details now in the museum at Tripoli (Fig.14.3). Light apparently entered through rock-cut windows or light-shafts in the south wall, and the painting of the vault took account of this. On a white ground a network of festoons and scrolls, delicately picked out in brown, forms large rectangular frames within which are figured panels; one of these larger elements can be reconstructed in its entirety with its central picture of Dionysus on a panther flanked by panels with female masks, running antelopes and a seaside village (Pls.14.3,4).[14] This last shows a set of six nearly identical houses beside a bay with shipping; two tidy trees and a walled garden remind us of the modern village of Zliten nearby, while the silhouette figures, standing and purposefully walking, and the running dog – all are worthy of a painting by L.S.Lowry. The walls were treated equally delicately but with simple architectural schemes in which a vertical movement prevails.[15] Here, for once, the perspective is perfectly understood and applied, while inset figured panels range in subject-matter from Hercules and Geryon to the inevitable pygmies and cranes. In the cool, indirect light this corridor must have been a veritable picture-gallery; and the best fragments now hang, appropriately, like pictures in the galleries of the Tripoli Museum – dancing and nereid figures, a Pegasus, a winged, palm-bearing Nike and – most bizarre of all – a green standing figure whose arms and bearing identify him as Mars. One partial figure, backed by a pale blue crescent moon, is that of Artemis-Selene (Diana-Luna). This arresting figure, sturdy in build and caught in a backward-looking glance, has much in common stylistically with the more flaccid, inebriated Dionysus nearby; she can be closely paralleled in a mosaic from Sabratha, but the closest similarity is with the mosaic of the four seasons at Zliten itself.[16] One is struck immediately by the large, heavily shaded eyes, the straight, firmly outlined nose and the solemn, down-turned mouth, the whole face

looking upwards to the right (or left, in the case of Spring, who is a
mirror-image of her sisters). If we need a more sophisticated and lifelike treatment of the same figure-type we might consider the torso of
Achilles on Scyros from the House of the Dioscuri at Pompeii;[17] a
detailed comparison, however, emphasises the individuality of treatment
in the Zliten faces. Does this mean, as Dorigo suggests,[18] "a personal
or professional coordination" between painter or mosaicist? Or are they
merely faithful executions of a late-antique stereotype by artists working in the same idiom? Or are the Seasons a deliberate imitation, some
two centuries or so later, of the paintings? These questions, or variations on them, have been debated at length by specialists who can find
support in works in many media, in many provinces and at varying periods.
But there is agreement on one point: that the Third Style paintings of
the *cryptoporticus* belong to the first century AD. Now the Seasons are
tile-mounted *emblemata* that could be imported, or may be re-used from
an earlier pavement in the house. Arguments for an early date for the
Seasons include the use of *opus sectile* and the nilotic scenes, both
of which fell from fashion in the late first or early second centuries;
and the head of Diana from Sabratha which lay below, and earlier than,
the Neptune head and could therefore be Hadrianic like the Baths themselves. So, although the style can indeed be paralleled in later works,
the earlier date is preferable - and it may still be possible to see the
mosaic *emblemata* and the wall-paintings as contemporary. A sequence for
the whole ensemble can be adapted from that of Dunbabin, namely:[19]

a) in the late first or early second century immigrant artists
   produced the mosaics of the acanthus volutes, the agricultural
   scenes, the amphitheatre and the paintings of the *cryptoporticus*.

b) between 150 and 175, local artists used the earlier *emblemata*
   in the Seasons mosaic.

c) at a considerably later date, some restoration work took place,
   notably the coarse nilotic mosaics, the mosaic of the agricultural
   scenes and reworking of others; it is possible that some work
   deliberately imitated earlier work, enhancing the difficulty of
   dating it on purely stylistic criteria.

d) the paintings of the Baths belong to a very late period.

     Nevertheless, even if we are looking at work of widely differing
periods, we can imagine that each addition to the ensemble was made with
reference to what was there already; the general impression is undoubtedly
that of "a coordinated if not unified conception of the decorative scheme
of the villa".[20]

     The Hunting Baths of Leptis Magna exemplify the characteristic
Roman interest in the interior of a building, as contrasted with the
exterior which in this case particularly was starkly functional and
unadorned. The building underwent one major and several minor modifica-
tions in its history from the late second century until perhaps AD 363
or so, and three major decorative phases can be detected (though some
had one or two, and room 4 had four).[21] These phases, though not perhaps
universally applicable, are an interesting guide to changing ideas in
décor. The *frigidarium* with its two apsidal plunges at the ends of a
long, barrel-vaulted room, shows these changes best. Its first phase
combined mosaic and stucco (plain and moulded); the vault was coffered,

with a central rosette, while the walls were covered in part, or even
entirely, with moulded stucco. Mosaics (marine, nilotic and mythological
scenes) were confined to the vaults of the apses and the lunette around
the head of each apse entrance. In the second phase even these mosaics
disappeared under a layer of painted plaster. In the third phase the
entire room was repainted, this time with the famous hunting scenes (a
lion-hunt on the north wall, a leopard - hunt on the south) and the
lower half of the walls veneered in marble. Interestingly, a geometric
floor mosaic was laid in a niche in the south wall. Each room has a
slightly different story to tell, warning us not to read too much
significance into the changes. For instance, while the mosaics in the
niches of room 2 were being plastered over, new mosaics were set in the
niches of the adjacent *piscina* (room 3) and under the arch to room 2;
conversely, in the next phase these mosaics were painted out while a
fresh niche mosaic was set in room 2 next door (in the floor). Likewise,
among the mosaics plastered over in room 2 was a nilotic scene, yet the
subsequent phase in room 3 was graced by two elaborate walls covered with
the same scenes. In other words, these detailed changes reflect not the
popularity or otherwise of mosaic and nilotic subject-matter but rather
a desire for consistency and coherence in the décor of particular rooms.
Nevertheless, some useful generalisations are possible: first, that
moulded stucco is limited to the earliest phase. Second, that vault-
and wall-mosaic give way to paint. And finally - an interesting contrast
to Campanian taste - imitation marble is common in the later phases. All
these phases are, unfortunately, not precisely datable, and indeed have
been disputed. But they probably range from the late second to the late
third centuries. The hunters' faces, which to the writer have much in
common with those from Sabratha and Zliten described above, have been
compared to the faces of Septimius Severus and his family in the famous
painted medallion in Berlin.[22]

These hunting scenes, at all events, are fairly late works, and
invite stylistic evaluation. First impressions, on entering the room,
are certainly in accord with those of Ward Perkins and Toynbee who
describe them as "full of life and vigorous movement".[23] However, a
prolonged consideration, when they are set beside other works in the
same vein, reveals their artistic limitations. Dorigo's comments may be
ungenerously harsh, but are nearer the mark; he describes them as
"stereotyped copies of both bodily and facial structure, industriously
and plausibly reproduced...shaped like puppets" and sees this art as
"complete fossilisation, in the sense of an absence of cultural and
stylistic contrast."[24] Yet they remain the most vivid scenes in a building whose patrons (supposedly a guild of *venatores*) spared no expense
but seemed satisfied, through successive redecorations of their premises,
with simple patterned walls, vaults and floors. For us, the interest of
this ensemble of simple walls and floors lies not in the ambitious
decoration of individual rooms but rather in its remarkable completeness;
we are at last able to study the decorative scheme of a small building
in its entirety, and moreover to document the minor adjustments through
time demanded by those who had to use it.

By the second half of the fourth century, in Tripolitania the ideas
and images of previous centuries were still current, and the powerful
influence of the Tetrarchy in their treatment can still be felt some
generations later. We can see this today in the well preserved double
tomb at Ghirgaresh, the so-called 'Mithraic Tomb'.[25] The name - which
may be a misnomer - was inspired by the painted inscriptions on the

plastered tomb-chests that occupied two of the four *loculi* and which were intact on discovery. We cannot now check the readings, which were, on that of Aelia Arisuth (the dominant tomb) *QUAE IACET LEA* and on that of her husband (?), Aelios son of Iuranthus, *QUI IACET LEO*. Initiates they may conceivably have been, but there is nothing overtly Mithraic about the extensive decorations around them. The individual elements - reclining genii with torches inverted, the peacock and the vine with birds perching in it (for resurrection and the afterlife), the chariot race - these are age-old symbols that by now may have been trite, though none the less valid. The chariot-race in particular is a fine specimen showing the course with its two *metae* and the four chariots, one for each of the four racing colours. Blue is winning, white has come to grief, green reins to avoid his crashed competitor and red brings up the rear. Between the red and green chariots a blue *jubilator* carries the prize vase towards the winner. Blue, we must infer, was Arisuth's colour, who has run and won the race of life.

It is her portrait that greets us on entry - a solemn but powerful figure in a plain white headdress and mantle relieved only by a plaited gold necklace. The circular *imago* is framed by a jewelled wreath supported by two stocky winged females whose execution is markedly inferior. The searching intensity of her expression anticipates the late Roman figures of the catacombs of Rome and the imagery of Byzantine times; but for contemporary masterpieces in the same genre we need search no further than the mummy portraits of the Fayyum. On either side of her tomb stand painted acolytes, each with a lighted torch. In them the artistic current of the Tetrarchy is still running strongly, for they might have stepped straight from one of the Piazza Armerina mosaics. Each wears the white dalmatic with embroidered panels and sleeves and a lozenge-in-circle badge at the bottom of the garment. Over the left shoulder hangs a white cloak with embroidered detail. The pose, with one foot firmly planted, the other lingering, is formal but attentive; the two uniformed retainers stand eternally alert for their mistress' command.

We return finally to the Mosaic of the Acanthus Volutes from Zliten, noted above, and to a significant detail that can easily escape notice. The grace and richness of this tour de force can be appreciated only on inspection in the Tripoli Museum, though part can be conveniently studied in Dunbabin 1978 pl.I,2. The tesserae are truly minute (up to 63 per sq.cm. showing that the miniature art of *opus vermiculatum* could, in the right hands, be used successfully on the grand scale. But the rich gradations of colour make this more akin to painting - a comment whose significance is clear when we look at the whole surviving fragment.[26]
For at the very edge, projecting into the floor from the foot of the wall, are four feet - two human, and two cloven hooves. This can mean only one thing: that on the wall, and presumably in paint (though we shall never be certain) stood two figures, perhaps a nymph and a satyr. The floor and the wall were thus united in a manner that has no parallel in the Roman world. Nowhere shall we find a better demonstration of an artist's conception of unity in the décor of a room; and nowhere - dare we suggest it? - a more subtle indication of that quality so often suppressed - a sense of humour.

ACKNOWLEDGEMENT

Thanks are due to Professor G. Caputo, Florence for permission to use material from S.Aurigemma, *l'Italia in Africa. Tripolitania* I, part 2.

NOTES

1. See Dunbabin 1978:235-7 for a review of this problem.

2. Aurigemma 1960, pl.3.

3. Aurigemma 1962, pl.25.

4. Aurigemma 1960, pls.83-86.

5. Aurigemma 1962, pl.68.

6. Ward Perkins and Toynbee 1951:183, pl.44.

7. Aurigemma 1960:100 *et seq*

8. E.g. ibid pl.113.

9. Ibid pl.120

10. Ibid pl.112.

11. Wheeler 1966 pl.18.

12. Dunbabin 1978 pl.1.

13. Aurigemma 1960 pl.161 *et seq.*

14. Ibid pl.24 *et seq.*

15. Ibid pl.66.

16. The comparison can be seen in Dorigo 1971, pls. 25-27.

17. Maiuri 1953:73.

18. Dorigo 1971:55.

19. Dunbabin 1978:237.

20. Dorigo 1971:50.

21. Ward Perkins and Toynbee 1950:178 *et seq.*

22. Ibid:192.

23. Ibid:181.

24. Dorigo 1971:208-9.

25. Toynbee 1965:121.

26. Aurigemma 1926, pl.160).

BIBLIOGRAPHY

Aurigemma, S., 1926. *I Mosaici di Zliten*, Rome-Milan.

Aurigemma, S., 1960. *L'Italia in Africa - Tripolitania: I. I Monumenti d'Arte Decorativa*. Part I: *I Mosaici*, Rome.

Aurigemma, S., 1962. Part 2: *Le Pitture d'Eta Romana*, Rome.

Di Vita, A., 1964. 'Questione di metodo' *Arch. Class* 16, 1964:315-318.

Di Vita, A., 1966. *La Villa della 'Gara delle Nereidi' presso Tagiura*. *Libya Antiqua* Suppl. II, 1966:46-61.

Dorigo, W., 1971. *Late Roman Painting*, London.

Dunbabin, K.M.D., 1978. *The Mosaics of Roman North Africa*, Oxford.

Maiuri, A., 1953. *Roman Painting*, Geneva.

Romanelli, P., 1972. 'Tomba romana con affreschi del IV secolo d.c. nella regione di Gargaresch-Tripoli' *Notizario Archeologico del Ministero delle Colonie* 3, 1922:21ff.

Toynbee, J.M.C., 1965. *The Art of the Romans*.

Ward-Perkins, J.B. and Toynbee, J.M.C., 1951. 'The Hunting Baths at Lepcis Magna' *Archaeologia* 93, 1951:165-195.

Wheeler, R.E.M., 1966. *Roman Africa in Colour*, London.